LECTURES

ON

CHRISTIAN DOCTRINE.

LECTURES

ON

CHRISTIAN DOCTRINE.

BY

ANDREW P. PEABODY,

PASTOR OF THE SOUTH CHURCH, PORTSMOUTH, N. H.

NEW EDITION,

WITH AN INTRODUCTORY LECTURE ON THE SCRIPTURES.

BOSTON AND CAMBRIDGE:

JAMES MUNROE AND COMPANY.

M DCCC LVII.

CAMBRIDGE: THURSTON AND TORRY, PRINTERS.

PREFACE.

These Lectures were prepared for the pulpit, without the slightest reference to their publication. They have been sent to the press as first written, at the urgent solicitation of many of the author's parishioners. They are not offered to the public, as a full compend of Christian doctrine, or as a fair exhibition of the *positive* side of the author's own faith; but simply as a discussion of the prominent points at issue between the Unitarian and the Calvinistic portion of the Christian Church. As such, they were deemed valuable and satisfactory by those who heard them; and it is hoped that they will prove so to those who may read them. To the Parish, whose uniformly kind and indulgent appreciation of his services and labors he is happy thus to acknowledge, they are respectfully and affectionately inscribed by

THE AUTHOR.

Portsmouth, N. H., Jan., 1844.

CONTENTS.

INTRODUCTORY LECTURE.

THE SCRIPTURES.*

2 TIMOTHY III. 16.

ALL SCRIPTURE IS GIVEN BY INSPIRATION OF GOD, AND IS PROFITABLE FOR DOCTRINE, FOR REPROOF, FOR CORRECTION, FOR INSTRUCTION IN RIGHTEOUSNESS.

IN the present Lecture, designed to be preliminary to a series of discourses on Christian doctrine, I shall present and defend my view of the authority of the Sacred Scriptures, and especially of the New Testament.

The Old Testament consists of *thirty-nine* separate books, all of them originally written in Hebrew, by nearly as many different authors, and at intervals during a period, as is commonly supposed, of more than a thousand years. The New Testament consists of *twenty-seven* books, written originally in Greek, by *ten* different authors, in the interval between the reputed date of our Saviour's ascension, and the close of the first century. These last books I shall

* The substance of this Lecture, originally delivered from the pulpit, was published in the Christian Examiner for May, 1842.

quote in the following Lectures as of plenary authority on all matters of Christian doctrine, while I shall also make occasional reference to the Old Testament, as indicating the divine mind with reference to the fundamental principles of religion.

We have a superabundant weight of external and internal evidence to convince us, that the books of the Old and New Testament (with unimportant exceptions) were written by the men whose names they bear, or at the times when, and the places where, they purport to have been written; that they were written honestly and in good faith; that they have in all times been regarded with reverence and confidence by those, who have enjoyed the best means of knowing their true character; and that the books of the New Testament were, most or all of them, written by the personal companions and followers of Jesus of Nazareth, or by their immediate disciples and friends. Now, were the Bible merely a series of historical works, or did it relate to matters of secondary interest and moment, we should be fully satisfied with this ample proof of the genuineness and authenticity of the several books which it contains. But the most honest men are liable to error, especially in quoting the sayings of others on abstract and spiritual subjects; and on subjects of this kind a very slight misrecollection might materially pervert the sense of what was uttered. How know we, then, but that the evangelists, though honest men, may, by the frailty of their own understandings and memories, have grossly misrepresented the language and spirit of Jesus? Some of these books, too, are not in a narrative form, but didactic and doctrinal; and, if they were written by fallible, yet honest men, without any peculiar illumination from heaven, how know we, that they are always sound in their counsels and right in their judgments? How can we assure ourselves, that they have not erred widely on matters both of doctrine and duty, as have many wise and honest men before and since?

These questions throw open the whole subject of inspiration; and it may be well for us to enter upon our inquiry with just notions of its magnitude. How much then does it involve? Does it cover the whole ground between Christian faith and infidelity? By no means. Whoever receives the history of Jesus as authentic, has within his reach enough of unquestionable truth to serve as the basis of Christian character. No one can believe the evangelists to have been honest men, without believing the principal facts in the life of Jesus and the essential doctrines of his religion. But the difference lies here. He, who regards the sacred writers as divinely inspired, deems himself possessed of an unerring guide as to all the minutiæ of doctrine, of an infallible compass for his whole path in life. His only question is, 'What say the law and the testimony?' That settled, he need seek no farther. He, on the other hand, who denies inspiration, while he would feel satisfied with regard to great truths, might be uncertain as to many lesser, yet important points; might often doubt whether the apostles spoke after the mind of Christ, or uttered their own fallible judgments; and thus, where the voice of Scripture was entirely clear, might be painfully perplexed as to the way of truth and duty.

But what is *inspiration?* We mean by this word, in its application to the Scriptures, *a divine influence exerted upon the minds of the sacred writers, to aid them in the exhibition of truth, and to save them from hurtful error.* No one, we presume, at the present day, would maintain that the very words of Scripture were dictated by the divine spirit; that the genealogies in the first book of Chronicles were breathed from heaven into the author's mind; or that there was anything supernatural in Paul's sending for his cloak and parchment. We observe in each of the sacred writers peculiarities, and sometimes imperfections of style, such as would naturally grow out of his education, mode of life, and temperament. Amos, the herdsman of Tekoah, writes in a much simpler style, and with a much greater affluence of rural imagery, than Isaiah and Ezekiel, whose condition in life seems to have differed widely from his. How easy is it to trace the impetuous Peter, the modest and affectionate John, the glowing and devoted Paul, in their respective writings! But, if the words of the Bible were dictated by God, instead of this great diversity of style, we should expect to see the whole Bible written in one unvarying style of unique grandeur. This strict verbal inspiration would detract greatly from the value of some portions of Scripture, particularly of the devotional parts; for their worth consists in their being expressions of devout feeling on the part of their authors, — upbreathings of hearts touched with a living coal from God's altar, and enabled to light a kindred flame in other souls, and thus to furnish examples and forms for the devotion of all coming times. We doubt not that the Jewish minstrels drank deeply from the same fountain of inspiration, from which the prophets drew their marvellous foreknowledge; but, if God dictated the very words of the Psalms, they cease to be specimens of human devotion, and appropriate models for man, and present to us the solecism of the Almighty praying to himself, and chanting his own praises. As to the merely historical parts of the Bible, if the authors knew, either by revelation, by their own observation and experience, or by means of authentic documents already extant, the facts which they related, they had no need of verbal inspiration to enable them to tell their stories faithfully. Moreover, on him, who should maintain the necessity of verbal inspiration for the original writers of the Old and New Testament, would rest the burden of showing, why like inspiration is not equally necessary for all *translators* of the Bible. In fact, the question of verbal inspiration, did it admit of being agitated, would be barely one of vain curiosity. It has ceased to be of any practical moment, since the Hebrew and the Greek became dead languages.

But while we believe that the sacred writers wrote each in his own style, and with a large degree of freedom, we maintain, that they were inspired, that their minds were preternaturally enlightened and guided, that holy men wrote as they were moved by the Holy Spirit. For, in the first place, the idea of inspiration is in strict accordance with reason and intrinsic probability. We cannot deny to the Father of man's spirit that power of direct and recognized communication with it, which he has granted to fellow men. We cannot suppose that God has opened the soul to the inbreathings of other souls, and left no avenue for the entrance of his own voice. No. If man has a soul, God must have the key to its every apartment, and must needs have at his command even those modes of access and forms of speech, which, for good reasons, he rarely sees fit to use.

Again, we believe that miracles were wrought for the establishment of Judaism and Christianity. Why is it less probable, that miracles should have been wrought for the faithful transmission of their records? If to plant the reign of truth and righteousness upon the earth was an object of sufficient moment to disturb the laws, which nature had for ages kept, surely to perpetuate that same reign on the solid basis of infallible testimony, was an object amply worthy of the equally magnificent, though less conspicuous miracle of inspiration.

We are also predisposed to believe in the inspiration of the sacred writers by the conscious wants of our own natures. We feel the need, not only of a generally faithful guide, but of one that we can trust as to all the details of truth and duty, — of records, which shall be to us, in things pertaining to godliness and a life to come, what a parent's words are to the confiding ear of infancy. We cannot bear to be left in doubt on subjects so momentous, even in their least imposing aspects. The infallibility of Jesus himself affords no sufficient basis for implicit, childlike faith, if those who recorded his sayings and pencilled the first developments of his truth, were liable to the common mistakes of unlettered and inexperienced biographers and interpreters. Our Jesus is the Jesus of their gospels and epistles; and it matters little, that the living person bore the express image and uttered the express words of God, if they were liable to gross error in painting that image and recording those words.

But it may be asked: 'Is there no basis for the plenary authority and virtual infallibility of the sacred writers, short of their inspiration in a peculiar and exclusive sense? To say nothing in this connection of the Old Testament, if the apostles were honest men, may we not rely upon them as amply competent, without supernatural aid, to have been both the biographers and the expositors of Jesus? They were long with him; must not every principle of his religion have so stamped itself upon their hearts; must not his spirit have so permeated their whole mental and moral being, as to take away the very power of mistake or failure? Must not their familiarity with him have done for them all that express inspiration could have done?' I reply, that, in the connection of the apostles with our Saviour, there were many circumstances, which seemed to render some subsequent illumination necessary, in order to their being faithful historians and expositors. From our Saviour's baptism to his ascension, there was the space of only sixteen months; and, though his principal disciples were with him at intervals during the whole of this time, there intervened but seven months between the call of the twelve and the ascension; and, even for a part of that period, they were absent from him on their mission among the villages, whither he was to follow them. Much of their intercourse with him was in the distracting presence of multitudes, much of it at times of fatigue, persecution, want, and fear. And, what is more to the point, according to their own account, they were ignorant of his true character till after his ascension. On the very ascension morning, they asked him, 'Lord, wilt thou at this time restore the kingdom to Israel?' They must therefore have listened to him all along with erroneous impressions. They understood not a large part of what he said, at the time when he uttered it. His true glory was veiled from them, while they were with him. They saw and heard through a false medium, and could not, therefore, in all cases have derived true and just ideas from what they saw and heard. But what men misunderstand they are prone to misremember, and, however honestly and unconsciously, to misrepresent; nor, when they get the right key to conversations and events, which they have once misunderstood, is it easy to apply it to them retrospectively, so as to restore them in their original fulness and significancy, and to make them in their own minds and in the narration of them to others, just what they would have been had they possessed the key at the outset. According to the common laws of mind, the New Testament must have been tinged throughout by the early misapprehensions of its authors, and must have presented in biography and in doctrine a double, a Janus-faced image, made up of the temporal Messiah, whom the apostles at first expected, and of that spiritual Redeemer, with whom, after the ascension, they ascertained that they had lived and walked. We thus should have had insufficient and unsatisfying Scriptures. But this is not the case. The only vestiges of these misapprehensions are in the repeated record of the fact, that they existed. Both biography and doctrine are of one shape and hue,— present a fabric entire and seamless as the Saviour's own tunic, and are, throughout, adapted to the higher views of their Master's mission and character, which ensued upon his departure from earth. Now this fact constitutes to my mind, in behalf of the inspiration of the writers of the New Testament, a presumptive argument too strong to be passed by without notice, though, in introducing the subject, I intended to speak only of the necessity for inspiration growing out of the misapprehensions, which existed during our Saviour's lifetime

For the reasons which I have stated, religious books written by inspired men are within the range of antecedent probability, and of reasonable expectation and desire. But how far should we antecedently expect the inspiration of the sacred writers to extend? So far, I reply, as is needful 'for doctrine, reproof, correction, and instruction in righteousness,' — so far as is necessary to afford an infallible guide in matters of religious faith and duty. Up to this point we should expect, at least for the sacred writers of the latter and more perfect dispensation, plenary inspiration. But here inspiration must cease. We should not expect to see miracles wrought (and inspiration is a miracle) for other than religious ends; for no lower ends seem of sufficient moment to outweigh the advantages resulting from an undisturbed course of nature. We may, therefore, consistently with the highest views of religious inspiration, suppose that the sacred writers were left to their own wisdom and research, with regard to such merely secular details as were within their reach; that they copied from ancient chronicles, compiled their genealogies from previously existing tables, and trusted to their own unaided memories for those minute and incidental circumstances, which had no religious bearing. This theory of inspiration may also be reconciled with any alleged imperfection of style in the sacred writings, with the slight discrepancies between the gospel narratives, with scientific inaccuracies in the Old and New Testament, in fine, with whatever objections have any other than a strictly religious aspect. While we would contend that, in a religious point of view, plenary inspiration pervades these records, we would regard and criticize them in every other aspect, as the writings of men of like passions, infirmities, and errors with other men of their own times and nation.

I now proceed to consider the positive grounds, on which this idea of inspiration rests. Let us first look at the New Testament.

The following are some of our Lord's promises to his apostles before his death: 'I will pray the Father, and he will give you another helper, even the spirit of truth.' * 'He will guide you into all truth.' 'He will take of mine and shew it unto you.' † 'He shall teach you all things, and bring all things to your remembrance, whatsoever I have said unto you.' ‡ Here is an express promise of two things, first, of a supernatural enlightening of the minds of the apostles with regard to religious truth; and, secondly, of a supernatural quickening of their recollections, with regard to what Jesus had said while he was with them. If the above quoted words of Jesus do not mean as much as this, they mean nothing. But the scene, at which they were uttered, was too solemn and too sad for unmean-

* John xiv. 16, 17. † John xvi. 13, 14. ‡ John xiv. 26.

ing hyperbole. The Master was just leaving his frail and trembling company of apostles, and professed to be giving them precepts and promises for their guidance and comfort when he should have gone from them; and it is a gross insult upon his spirit to maintain, that, at such a season, he should have fed them upon the wind, should have made a parade of oriental metaphor, and employed words, which literally denote a divine inspiration, to express no more than must happen to them according to the common laws of mind. But were the recollections of Matthew and John thus miraculously quickened? Then may we cherish the undoubting assurance, that Jesus was, said, and did all that they represent him to have been, said, and done. Was the whole system of Christian doctrine and duty thus preternaturally laid open to John and James, Peter and Jude? Did the spirit of truth guide them into all truth, as Jesus had promised them? Then may we rest assured, that their epistles contain neither doctrines nor precepts of man's device, but the truth and the will of God. We may trace also in these epistles a consciousness of inspiration. For instance, Peter thus classes himself and his fellow apostles with the prophets, to whom we well know that they ascribed divine inspiration. 'That ye may be mindful of the words, which were spoken before by *the holy prophets*, and of the commandments of *us, the apostles of the Lord and Saviour.'* *

Paul was not one of the twelve; but, if he was a sane and an honest man, he was equally inspired with them. He repeatedly, and in a great variety of forms, professes inspiration. Such is undeniably the import of passages like the following: 'The gospel, which was preached of me, is not after man; for I neither received it of man, nor was I taught it but by the revelation of Jesus Christ.' † 'Which things we teach, not in the words which man's wisdom teacheth, but in the words which the holy spirit teacheth.' ‡ 'If any man think himself to be a prophet or spiritual, let him acknowledge that the things, which I write unto you, are the commandments of the Lord.' § Again, speaking of his system of doctrine, Paul says: 'Ye received it not as the word of men, but, as it is in truth, the word of God.' || And again, in a similar connection: 'He that despiseth, despiseth not man, but God, who hath also given unto us his holy spirit.' ¶ Now let him, who thinks that St. Paul intended to express, by words like these, only the fact, that he had the same kind of inspiration which every good man has, try the case, by supposing any good man of his acquaintance to use similar language. Would not any man, of however

* 2 Peter iii. 2. † Gal. i. 11, 12. ‡ 1 Cor. ii. 13.
§ 1 Cor. xiv. 37. || 1 Thess. ii. 13. ¶ 1 Thess. iv. 8.

high spiritual attainments, who in our day should talk thus about himself, be regarded by every sober mind, as either an impostor or a madman? These passages either mean nothing, or they denote *divine inspiration* in the special and exclusive sense of the words; and, if St. Paul was an honest man, and in full possession of his mental faculties, he was an inspired man.

There remain two of the evangelists, Mark and Luke, who were not apostles, who were not included in the Saviour's promise of divine illumination, and who make no professions of inspiration; who therefore may have been honest and faithful writers, without having been inspired. What shall we say of them? The question of their inspiration is of secondary importance; for,

1. Mark's gospel contains hardly anything not to be found in Matthew's or John's; and Luke's additional matter, though considerable in amount, and of intense interest, could lay the foundation for no new doctrine or principle, but harmonizes entirely, in tone and spirit, with the narrative of the apostolic evangelists.

2. Though these two gospels do not bear the names of apostles, they were virtually apostolic productions. Mark was the intimate companion of Peter, and a tradition almost as old as his gospel, and handed down without dispute, informs us that he wrote by Peter's dictation.

Luke distinctly avows himself, in the proem of his gospel, to be only the penman of what he had received directly from the apostles:—'Even as they delivered them unto us, which from the beginning were eye-witnesses and ministers of the word.'* As for the Acts of the Apostles, a large part of the book is mere history, and the record of scenes and events of which Luke was an eye-witness. There is good reason to suppose, that he was present at the miracle of the cloven tongues, on the day of Pentecost; and in the latter part of the book, he expressly speaks of himself as St. Paul's travelling companion, and in this part is evidently copying from a diary. There can exist no doubt, as to his competency to write a history of affairs, in which he had so deep a personal interest, especially as, unlike the apostles during our Saviour's lifetime, he understood the religion, of which he was writing the history, and therefore saw things from the true point of view. Equally little doubt can there be, as to the decisive internal marks of accuracy and faithfulness, which this book presents.

Yet it seems to me highly probable, that Mark and Luke were inspired men; for,

1. We have reason to believe, that miraculous gifts and endowments were not confined to the apostles; and on whom else can we so readily

* Luke i. 2.

suppose that they would have been bestowed, as on the intimate and confidential friends of such men as Paul and Peter?

2. We find that, from the earliest times, Mark's and Luke's writings were regarded by the Church as of equal worth and authority with those of Matthew and John.

The internal character of the New Testament strongly confirms the view, which we have taken, of the inspiration of its writers. Its style and tone befit men, whom a divine spirit had lifted above the passions and prejudices of the multitude. The completeness of their works, viewed collectively, may be regarded as a presumptive argument of great weight in favor of their inspiration. We know not how sufficiently to admire the divine skill displayed by the evangelists. They are relating the godlike pilgrimage, works, and words of one, who came from God and went to God,—of one, who stood out alone, of all beings that ever trod the earth, in the loftiness of his character, in the sanctity and vastness of his mission. Their narrative is brief,—it is crowded full with marvel and miracle,—it tells us throughout of heavenly things. Yet, without ever forgetting the heaven-descended, the son of God, they present to us, on almost every page, a section of our Saviour's domestic life and walk among men, show him to us as a son and a brother, as a neighbor and a friend, as a master and a citizen, among kindred, among strangers, among enemies, in the temple, at the marriage feast, in the house of mourning. In this wide diversity of detail, we see always the same majestic and godlike image, in no circumstances, however narrow or humble, shorn of a ray of its glory. And when the authors confess that, while the divine original was upon the earth, they knew him not, we cannot help believing, that the image was reproduced, and sustained before their inward vision, by the spirit of God. We cannot help drawing a similar inference from the general character of the epistles. They relate, for the most part, to local and temporary questions, and disputes, and to a great diversity of these, many of them difficult, mixed, complex cases. Yet who will venture to maintain, that these writers have, in a single instance, failed to apply to the solution of these cases the true spirit of Christ, and the strict law of righteousness? On the other hand, all their decisions are in entire accordance with each other, and with the spirit that breathes through the gospels; and with the discussion of questions, that have passed away forever, they have connected so many maxims of eternal truth, and so many clear and expanded illustrations of great and everlasting principles, that these epistles must needs go down to the end of time, in the connection in which they now stand with the gospels, as the best commentary upon them, and as an exhaustless repertory of Christian wisdom.

These considerations are greatly strengthened by one of a negative character. There is in the New Testament nothing which militates against our faith in the inspiration of its authors, — no brand of falsehood or folly to suggest an opposite theory, — nothing superficial or shallow; but a profoundness and fulness which no created mind has exhausted or outgrown. No man, whom men have consented to call wise, has professed himself to have advanced, in ethical or religious culture, beyond the New Testament; but the wisest men have found in it enough to stretch and task their highest powers through the whole of life. But what unaided man had written, we might expect man to exhaust or outgrow. Taking our view of inspiration for a stand-point, we could not expect to find the New Testament more perfect, or, in any essential respect, other than it is; — it is just such a collection of books as this theory would presuppose.

Add to this consideration, the wide, the almost inconceivable contrast between the books of the New Testament and the residue of the early Christian writings extant, some of which bear the names of personal friends and followers of the apostles, and, whether genuine or not, must belong to the age next succeeding the apostolic.

The most edifying of these contain much that is puerile and absurd, — much that would settle in the negative, without dispute or division, the question whether their authors were inspired. The highest degree of veneration, which has ever been paid to the New Testament, cannot separate it from the best other writings of the primitive days of the Church, by broader marks of distinction, than show themselves on the very face of the respective works. And yet, had the writers of the New Testament been left without any greater degree of divine illumination, than these other writers had, we can hardly believe, that so very decisive marks of difference would have been presented.

You will perceive, that I make the souls of the apostles and evangelists, and not the parchment on which they wrote, the seat of inspiration. I by no means assert, that the books of the New Testament received their outward shape, or even their existence, from a divine monition, urging one to write a gospel, and another an epistle. I suppose that they wrote as they saw the churches to need, and were guided by their own judgment as to what and when they should write. But they were men taught of the spirit, — guarded against error, and furnished with adequate views of truth and duty, by inspiration from on high; and out of the abundance within, they both spake and wrote. There was the same inspiration in their oral instructions. There was the same inspiration in whatever else they may have written, which has not come down to us. There would have been the same inspiration in the writings (had they left us any) of Philip or Bartholomew, of Lebbeus or Simon the Canaanite. The exigencies of the case, and the testimony of the apostles themselves, convince us that they all (and those immediately associated with them also) were inspired men; and the New Testament has come down to us, as the only surviving records of what was written under the influence of that inspiration.

We come now to consider the inspiration of the writers of the Old Testament. In vindicating their inspiration, we are called upon to defend only the religious character of the Old Testament. Is its general history defective and untrustworthy? We think not; but, if it be so, this fact touches not the question of inspiration. Are its genealogies imperfect, and inconsistent with each other? We are rather amazed that they should be so full and coherent; but, were they drawn out with the minute accuracy of modern heraldry, we should not claim supernatural aid for their compilation. Is Solomon's Song a mere epithalamium? If so, we do not believe that Solomon had any divine assistance in writing it. Are there many portions of the

Old Testament, where the writers show themselves independent of peculiar divine guidance, and subject to the prejudices and errors of their times? Be it so. We should antecedently expect the penman of the earlier, and less perfect dispensation, to have been endowed with a less intense and pervading inspiration; to have lived less constantly in the perception of spiritual truth; to have had only transient glimpses, where the apostles enjoyed open vision. We should antecedently expect to find more of the merely human element in the earlier Scriptures, which were designed to be but as 'a light shining in a dark place, until the day should dawn and the day-star arise.' The question of inspiration should be discussed solely with reference to the religious contents of the Old Testament. The question is, whether those things in the Jewish Scriptures, which were beyond man's knowledge or foresight, or far above the light of those times, were discoveries, speculations, happy guesses, or whether they were actually derived from the inspiration of God.

Among the internal marks of the inspiration of the writers of the Old Testament, we would first name the religious unity and harmony, which pervade it. The writers all have the same conception of God, of devotion, of duty. This has not generally been the case among the less cultivated nations. The Jupiter of Homer differs from the Jupiter of the later Greek tragedians. The popular conceptions of every personage in the Pantheon of Greek mythology were gradually developed, and essentially modified by time. On the other hand, the Jehovah of Moses, Isaiah, and Malachi, at intervals of many centuries, during which vast revolutions had been wrought in the national condition and culture, is one and the same Jehovah. The conception reached the highest form, which language could give it, in the writings of Moses, nay, in the very name *Jehovah;* and in that form it remained fixed, until Jesus softened it with warmer beams of fatherly love. Nor yet can we trace any diversity among these writers, as to the way in which God is to be worshipped, or the duties which he requires.

The frequent loftiness of thought and style in the Old Testament, beyond all other ancient writings, lifting the soul, as it were, into the very presence-chamber of the Deity, sustains the idea, that these majestic passages were written by men, whose spirits had been elevated and expanded by special nearness of converse with the Divine Being. There are portions of Isaiah and Ezekiel, there are some of the Psalms of David, which are, to the devout ear, more like a voice from heaven, than like the words of man.

In fine, the Old Testament stands out in such

a prominent contrast to all other equally ancient writings extant, even to the writings of the wisest and best men in the most cultivated ages, that we know not how to account for its sublime theology, its clear and high views of duty, its pervading tone of confidence and authority, except by ascribing to its authors special illumination from the spirit of God. We cast our eyes over the brightest pages of profane literature, and find nowhere a view of the divine nature, on which we can repose; but see the mind distracted among a multitude of clashing deities, bowed down by the spirit of fear and trembling, dreading the thunderbolt without ever trusting the love of the divinity, cringing before gods, possessed of all human, and worse than human, passions and infirmities. We then turn to the Bible, and we read: 'The Lord is my shepherd: I shall not want. He maketh me to lie down in green pastures; he leadeth me beside the still waters. Though I walk through the valley of the shadow of death, I will fear no evil, for thou art with me; thy rod and thy staff, they comfort me.' Now all the logic in the world can never convince me, that we are indebted solely to that old barbarous king, of a nation unlettered and unrefined, for these sentiments, which anticipate the very spirit of Jesus; which express all, and more than all, that the most pious heart can feel;

which will still be the burden of our song, when, beyond the reach of earthly infirmity, 'the Lamb who is in the midst of the throne shall feed us, and shall lead us unto living fountains of waters.' We might make similar remarks with regard to very many passages, which present glimpses of God, of truth, and of duty, which, our hearts tell us, are the very highest of eternal verities, and which stand entirely alone in the literature of the world before Christ, both as to their depth and fulness of meaning, and as to the tone of majestic and simple confidence, in which they are announced.

The numerous fulfilled prophecies, contained in the Old Testament, offer a more tangible, though hardly a stronger proof of the inspiration of its writers, than the traits to which we have already referred. I have not time to discuss these prophecies. They cover a large portion of human history. The fulfilment of some of them can be distinctly traced in the past; that of others is now in progress, and known and read of all men. The present condition of the Hebrew nation could hardly be described, in many of its distinctive and unprecedented features, with more accuracy, by a modern geographer, than we find it foretold in the Old Testament. Could blind chance have conjured into being phantoms of poetic fancy, that should thus correspond to actual events across the gulf of ages? Could she have brought together, and worked into the brains of those old seers just the same elements, which after many centuries Providence would embody in the counsels and destinies of nations? This is harder to believe, than that she could paint a flower, or blunder a world into being. The recurrence of the same harmonies at distant intervals, in the sphere-music of time, can be accounted for, only by supposing the harmony to have been first struck by the same omnipotent hand that repeats it.

We have also, in favor of the inspiration of the writers of the Old Testament, the testimony of the infallible Jesus and of his inspired apostles. Jesus says, 'Search the Scriptures; for in them ye think ye have eternal life; and they are they which testify of me,'* that is, which foretell me, which have a prophetic character,—a character which could result only from divine inspiration. And again, 'Had ye believed Moses, ye would have believed me; for he wrote concerning me,'† prophetically, of course. In like manner Jesus, epitomizing the whole Old Testament, speaks of what was written concerning him 'in the law of Moses, and in the prophets, and in the Psalms.'‡ He often

* John v. 39. † John v. 4. ‡ Luke xxiv. 44.

also quotes these writings as of divine authority and final appeal.

The apostles, also, continually quote the Old Testament as authoritative. St. Peter says: 'The prophecy came not in old time by the will of man; but holy men of God spake as they were moved by the holy spirit.'* Paul, too, writes to Timothy: 'All Scripture is given by inspiration of God, (or, more properly, *pervaded by a divine afflatus*,) and is profitable for doctrine, for reproof, for correction, for instruction in righteousness.'†

I have now shown, I trust, that the inspiration of the sacred writers rests on a firmer basis, than that of anile superstition. I am aware, that on this subject low and lax views often find favor. But to me faith on this point appears the part of sound philosophy. If God stands to us in the paternal relation, in which Jesus presents him, an intrinsic *a priori* probability attaches itself to any theory, in proportion as it brings him near to his children, and appeals to their implicit confidence. In a world not fatherless, for the short-sighted and frail children of an infinite Father, it is more philosophical to believe than to disbelieve in miracle and inspiration. The philosophy of the filial heart is higher and of vastly more worth than that of the doubting head.

* 2 Peter i 21 † 2 Tim. iii. 16.

Such are the views of inspiration, which lead me, on all subjects of religious doctrine and duty, to bow submissively to the authority of the written word; and, in this deference to the voice of Scripture, I have the entire and cordial sympathy of the great body of Unitarian Christians. Many of them were educated in a different creed; but have been made Unitarians solely by the diligent, prayerful study of the Bible. The Bible is our only confession of faith, — it is to us at once the pillar and the ground of the truth. But we contend for the right of appealing for authority on all controverted points to the Scriptures as originally written. Our common translation we regard as in the main accurate, — as generally representing the sense of the sacred writers. But our translators were uninspired and fallible men. They were many men, and endowed with different degrees of learning and acumen. They were the partisans of peculiar views of Christian truth and of ecclesiastical government. They were appointed to their work by a shallow-minded and pedantic monarch, who gave them in some respects express and peremptory rules of procedure, which they dared not violate. They lived also in the infancy of biblical criticism. Since their day, many ancient manuscripts of the New Testament have been brought to light, and collated with each other, and with the earliest versions, so that the Greek text, now received among critics of all denominations, presents not a few deviations from the 'received text,' so called, which was the basis of their translation. For these reasons, we must, in matters of controversy, sometimes appeal from the translation to the original. All Christian scholars do this. I shall make such appeals occasionally, though very seldom, in the following Lectures; but, when I refer to the original, it will not be to my own peculiar views, or to the views of any one denomination, as to what the text of the original ought to be. I shall always refer to the text of the original, as settled by the researches of learned men of various denominations, and as received by enlightened Christians of every portion of the Church.

With the views of Scripture now unfolded and explained, the question to be answered in the following Lectures is simply this: What testimony do the sacred writings, in their original form, and fairly interpreted, bear with reference to God, to Christ, and to the nature, duty, and destiny of man? My sole design and purpose is to reason from the Scriptures; my only object is to receive and to communicate the light of God's revealed word upon those departments of religious truth, on which Christians are the most widely at variance. And my sincere prayer for you and for myself is, that the Infinite Spirit of truth may guide us into all truth, and through the truth may redeem and sanctify us.

LECTURE I.

THE DIVINE NATURE.

EPHESIANS IV. 6.

ONE GOD AND FATHER OF ALL, WHO IS ABOVE ALL, AND THROUGH ALL, AND IN YOU ALL.

My object, in the course of lectures which I now commence, is to exhibit, so far as I am able, a fair and candid view of the points, on which most of us differ from other classes of Christians, and of the grounds, on which our peculiar views rest. In doing this, it will of course be necessary for me to make reference to the creeds of others; but such reference will be made as seldom as possible, in a spirit of unfeigned kindness, and, I trust, in a kindly tone and manner. My aim is, not controversy, but truth. I wish to aid you in the establishment of your own faith, not to furnish you with the means of attacking your neighbors. I wish to have you capable of maintaining and defending your views of Christian truth when they are assailed, and of instructing in them the young and inquiring; but should be exceedingly sorry to see among you that proselyting spirit, which would make incursions into other folds, or hurl the missiles of theological warfare at those who have adopted other modes of faith. Equally sorry should I be, that you should take any views of truth on my authority. Let me act only as your pioneer.

Our text implies the unity of God. This doctrine there is no need of our defending against Polytheism. But there has grown up in the Christian Church a doctrine, which, to those who reject it, seems as much opposed to the divine unity, as any form of Polytheism is. I mean the doctrine of the TRINITY. This will be my subject this evening. We will first inquire whether the Bible teaches, or implies, the view of the divine nature designated by this word; and, if it shall appear that the Bible teaches no such doctrine, we will then endeavor to ascertain whence it comes. I shall reserve for future lectures the arguments for and against the supreme divinity of our Saviour, and for and against the personality of the Holy Spirit, and shall confine myself this evening to the single point of *a threefold distinction in the divine nature.*

We ought at the outset to define the *Trinity* But here we are thrown into confusion; for hardly any two writers will agree upon the same definition. We may, however, classify the definitions given, and may thus show the different senses in which this doctrine has been professed and held.

1. There are many professed Trinitarians, particularly of the English Church, who maintain the supremacy of the first person of the Trinity, and the subordinate rank of the other two. This was the belief of Bishop Bull, who wrote much upon the subject, was called in England a Trinitarian, and was deemed an able defender of the creed of his own church, but whose writings would pass (and justly) as Unitarian, on this side of the Atlantic. Indeed, his is nearly the same doctrine, on account of which, Rev. Noah and Thomas Worcester, of our own State, were, thirty or forty years ago, cast out as heretics by their clerical brethren; and a singular fact it is, that, for similar views similarly expressed, Christian ministers should, on one side of the Atlantic, be crowned with fame and honor, in a Trinitarian church, as defenders of the faith, and on the other side should be compelled to take up the cross of persecution, and bear the reproach of heresy. But our American clergy were right. The second and third persons of the Trinity either are self-existent, or were created. If self-existent, they must needs be independent. Having within themselves the cause of their own existence, they must be complete and self-sufficient, so that they cannot have come into subjection to any other being. But, according to Bishop Bull, they are subordinate; and, if subordinate, they are not self-existent, but must have

been created, cannot then have existed from eternity, and therefore are not God. Bishop Bull, indeed, admits that they were derived from the divine essence, which is merely an obscure and involved way of saying, that they were created out of nothing.

2. There are others, (and they are very numerous in our own country,) who understand by the Trinity a threefold classification of the divine attributes. According to this view, God, being still one and the same being, in nature and providence, is called the Father,— in the work of redemption, the Son,—in his converting and sanctifying influences, the Holy Spirit. Thus we have God the Creator and Preserver, God manifest in the flesh, and God dwelling and working in the human soul; and these three, not separate beings, but the same being regarded in three different aspects. This is the view presented in that very popular doctrinal work, Abbott's Corner Stone; and, from the general acceptance which this book has found, I infer that this view of the Trinity is not deemed heretical. But it differs from Unitarianism only in name and in form of statement.

3. Another form, in which the Trinity has been held, supposes three distinct and equal divine minds united by a mutual consciousness of each other's volitions and acts. Sherlock, an eminent divine of the Church of England, says:

'To say that there are three divine persons, and not three distinct infinite minds, is both heresy and nonsense. The distinction of persons cannot be more truly and aptly represented, than by the distinction between three men; for Father, Son, and Holy Ghost, are as really distinct persons, as Peter, James, and John. We must allow the divine persons to be real, substantial beings.' Howe, the celebrated Calvinistic divine, speaks of the three divine persons as 'distinct, individual, necessarily existing, spiritual beings,' forming together 'the most delicious society.' This comes nearer an intelligible doctrine than most statements of the Trinity. But it sounds strangely like Tritheism; and I hardly know how those, who maintain it, can be said to believe in the unity of God.

4. There is another class of Trinitarians, probably the largest of all, who profess to believe the doctrine, without attempting to understand or explain it; that is, they hold the phraseology of the doctrine sacred, but attach no meaning to it. The nearest approach that they can make to a definition of the Trinity, is, to say that it is *three somewhats somehow united.*

Such are the various forms, in which the doctrine of the Trinity is held in the Christian Church, — forms so diverse from each other, that, were we to define the Trinity, so as to include the views of all who profess to believe in it, we could only say that it denotes God to be *both three and one.*

Let us now see whether the Bible teaches a Trinity. This doctrine, if it be true, is of the utmost interest and moment, and ought to mould and shape all our religious notions, and to be recognized in all our praises and our prayers. We should, therefore, expect to see it very clearly set forth in a revelation, purporting to come from God. But so far is this from being the case, that Trinitarians do not quote a single text as declarative of this prime article of their creed. They admit that it is nowhere distinctly stated in the Bible. Formerly, the three stories of Noah's ark, and the proverb, 'A threefold cord is not easily broken,' occupied a prominent place among Trinitarian proof-texts; but no one would think of using them now, and there remains not a single text from the Old Testament, which Trinitarians now cite as designating a threefold distinction in the divine nature.

There are, however, numerous instances, in which, when the Almighty is spoken of in the Hebrew Scriptures, a plural form is used, — sometimes a plural noun connected with a singular verb, — sometimes a plural pronoun with a plural verb, when God is represented as speaking in the first person. The Hebrew word in the Old Testament most frequently translated God, is *Elohim*, a plural noun, literally meaning *gods;* but it is usually connected with verbs in the singular, so as to indicate that but one person is denoted by the plural noun. There are also several instances in which we find such forms of speech as these: 'Let us make man in our image, after our likeness,' — 'Let us go down, and there confound their language.' Now though this form of speech has often been quoted to prove a plurality of persons in the divine nature, I can hardly conceive of its being quoted, with such a purpose, by any person moderately well acquainted with the Hebrew tongue. This plural form is a common Hebrew idiom, employed whenever anything of peculiar dignity or magnitude is spoken of. Grammarians call it the *plural of excellence* or *majesty;* and truly learned and candid Trinitarians admit that it is nothing more. Calvin, whose orthodoxy none will doubt, sets aside this argument for the Trinity. Professor Stuart, in his Hebrew Grammar, speaks of this form as simply denoting dignity or majesty, and as having no connection with the idea of plurality. Permit me to give you one or two examples of the way, in which this *plural of excellence* is employed. You all remember, in the book of Job, the description of the *behemoth*, by which is probably meant the *hippopotamus. Behemoth* is the plural of *behemah*, which means a *beast.* As used in Job, it is a plural noun joined with singular verbs and pronouns, and evidently means a *great beast;* and the hippopotamus was denoted by this indefinite word, expressing his vast size and strength, because there was no name for him in the Hebrew. The same plural form is used when false gods are spoken of. *Baalim* and *Ashtaroth* are plural nouns. 'The lords of the Philistines gathered them together, to offer a great sacrifice unto Dagon, their *god*,' literally *gods*.* The same plural word is used, when the Almighty says to Moses, 'See, I have made thee a *god*, literally *gods*, (*elohim*,) to Pharaoh.'† Where it is said that the butler and the baker 'had offended their *lord* the king of Egypt,'‡ the Hebrew word is *lords*, (one of the plural titles of the Almighty;) and so it is where Joseph's brethren say of him: 'The man who is the *lord*, literally, *lords*, of the land, spake roughly unto us.'§ Many of you well know what the Septuagint is, — a Greek translation of the Old Testament, made by learned Jews long prior to the Christian era. These Jews must of course have understood their own language, and must have known whether there was any mysterious signification couched in *Elohim*, and other kindred forms; but they invariably render these Hebrew plurals by Greek nouns in the singular, without any additional qualifying words.

* Judges xvi. 23. † Exodus vii. 1.
‡ Genesis xl. 1. § Genesis xlii. 30.

There is another consideration of great weight, with reference, not to this point alone, but to the Old Testament generally, and one which demonstrates beyond dispute, that the Trinity was not taught in the Jewish scriptures. It is this: the Jews, in general, both in ancient and modern times, have been opposed to this doctrine, have left no trace of it in their standard commentaries and religious works, and have resisted the use of their sacred writings in proof of it. There was indeed a seeming exception to this remark, in a numerous sect of Platonistic Jews, whose head-quarters were at Alexandria. They, in common with the later Platonists generally, maintained a Trinity, yet less as a theological than as a philosophical dogma, drawing their authority for it less from Moses and the prophets, than from Plato and his disciples, from whom, as I believe, it crept into the Christian Church. These Trinitarian Jews have had a few successors in more recent times. But to the Jews in general, the Trinity has been for ages, and still is, the greatest stumbling-block in the way of their conversion to Christianity. It is universally admitted, that a very large part of the early Jewish converts rejected the Trinity; and it is a striking and significant fact, that great numbers of the Jews continued to become Christians up to the date, when, as we believe, the Trinity was foisted into the Christian system, while, since that date, the conversion of a single Jew has been one of the rarest events.

These facts indicate that the Trinity could have formed no part of the Jewish revelation. But, if this were the case, we should expect to find this doctrine formally and explicitly announced in the New Testament, and occupying there the prominent place, which of right belongs to a radically new view of the divine nature. But how is this? It is not pretended that there is in the New Testament any express declaration of this doctrine; and there are quoted but two texts, in which the names of the three persons are said to be placed together in such a way, as strongly to imply a *trinity in unity*.

The text most relied on is the form of baptism '*in* or into *the name of the Father, and of the Son, and of the Holy Ghost* or Spirit.'* One would think, at first sight, that this form implied anything rather than three *equal* persons; for what mean the terms, *Father* and *Son?* If they mean anything, must they not denote the derived and subordinate existence of him, who is termed the Son? It is of no avail to call this an unsearchable mystery. The words *Father* and *Son*, as used in this connection, either mean something or nothing. If nothing, then does the Bible mock man's ignorance by the wanton use of words without meaning. But if they mean any-

* Matthew xxviii. 19

thing, they must at least denote that the Son owes his existence to a Father, therefore is not self-existent, and consequently is not God. Yet more, the words employed in this text to denote the *Holy Spirit* are, in the original, a neuter noun and adjective; and, though words in the neuter gender might naturally be used to signify a divine *influence*, we can hardly suppose that they would be selected to designate a divine *person.* It is said, that the sacred writers could not have thus connected unequal names? What shall we say then of this passage,—'All the congregation . . . . . worshipped the Lord and the king?'* Or of this,—'I charge thee before God, and the Lord Jesus Christ, and the elect angels?'† Is it said, that, baptism being a form of dedication, the sacred writers could not have connected with it any but divine names? I reply that the Israelites are said by St. Paul to have been 'baptized unto Moses,' ‡ and that he also speaks of the disciples of Christ as having been 'baptized into his death.' § In the former instance, men are said to be baptized unto one, who confessedly is not God; and in the latter, into what it must be admitted, is not a person.

The form of baptism depends not for its appropriateness on the doctrine of the Trinity. The infant or the convert, on being initiated

* 1 Chron. xxix. 20. † 1 Tim. v. 21
‡ 1 Cor. x. 2. § Rom. vi. 3.

into the Church of Christ, is most naturally and fittingly consecrated to the Father God, whom Jesus revealed and manifested, to the great Teacher himself, and to the regenerating and sanctifying influence from heaven, without which one cannot truly be a Christian.

The other Trinitarian proof-text is the apostolic benediction: 'The grace of the Lord Jesus Christ, and the love of God, and the communion of the Holy Ghost, be with you all.'* This proves nothing. Had a formal statement of the Trinity been here intended, the second person would not have been placed first. The obvious sense of the benediction is: 'May the favor of the great Head of the Church, the love of his God and our God, and the free and constant participation of his sanctifying influences, be yours forever.'

These are the only texts which Trinitarians in general cite as declarative of a threefold distinction in the divine nature. There still stands in our English Bible, a text, which more than implies the Trinity. It is this: 'There are three that bear record in heaven, the Father, the Word, and the Holy Ghost, and these three are one.'† It is now admitted, on all sides, that this verse formed no part of the original text of the New Testament. The highest authority for the text

* Cor. xiii. 14. † 1 John v. 7.

of the New Testament is that of ancient Greek manuscripts, of which several hundreds of either a whole or a part of the New Testament, bearing date from the fourth century down to the invention of the art of printing, have been examined and collated. No less than a *hundred and fifty* of these manuscripts contain the first epistle of John; but the text in question is not found in one of them. The next highest authority is that of manuscripts of ancient versions of the New Testament. This text is wanting in all of this class of manuscripts, except in those of the Vulgate Latin, and is wanting in all the earliest manuscripts, even of that. The next highest authority is that of the numerous Scriptural quotations of the earlier Christian writers. Now, none of the Greek fathers, who used the New Testament in its original, have quoted this text, or recognized its existence, no, not even in the height of the Arian controversy, when every text that could be made available was pressed into the service. This text was not printed in the earliest printed editions of the Greek Testament; and, when it was first printed, it was translated into the Greek from the Latin of the Vulgate, — the accredited version of the Romish Church. Erasmus, the greatest biblical scholar at the era of the Reformation, had published two editions of the New Testament without inserting this text. He was earnestly remonstrated with for omitting it; and his reply was, that he would insert it, if a single Greek manuscript containing it could be found. A manuscript was found and sent him, — a manuscript undoubtedly prepared for that express purpose, as there are no traces of its previous existence. He, to make his promise good, inserted the disputed text in his third edition; and it so happened that this third edition became the basis of the generally received Greek text, which was used by King James's translators. Such is the history of the only text in the Bible, which indisputably stands where it has no rightful place. But it occupies this place chiefly in editions and translations of the Vulgate, and in our common English Bibles. It is omitted in critical editions of the Greek Testament. Luther omitted it in his German Bible; Calvin spoke doubtingly of it; nor do I find a single critic or commentator, however orthodox, who leaves it unquestioned. Wardlaw, the most able champion of the Trinity within the range of my reading, says of this text: 'This text should have been entitled to hold the first place, if its genuineness had been undisputed, or disputed on slender grounds. I freely acknowledge, however, that the evidence of the spuriousness of this celebrated passage, if it were even much less conclusive than in my own mind it appears to be, would be quite sufficient to prevent me from resting upon it any part of the weight of my argument.'

So much for this text. But let me in connection with it, though rambling from my main object, say a word upon the certainty, which we enjoy, that the New Testament has come down to us substantially as it was at first written. These hundreds of manuscripts, these ancient versions, these numerous and copious quotations by the fathers of the church, constitute a vast array of witnesses, who all agree in testifying to the genuineness, sentence for sentence, and almost word for word, of the Christian Scriptures as we have them. To be sure, slips of the pen in transcribing have produced many slight differences, corresponding to the misprints in a printed book. But, in the whole of the New Testament, there is not a single sentence, not a single phrase of importance, and there are but *two* words of essential significance, with regard to which the vast majority of the witnesses do not agree.

You must, I think, see with me on how frail a foundation the Scriptural argument for the Trinity rests. There is one other consideration, to which I would allude with all possible brevity. The first person of the Trinity is termed the *Father;* but did it never occur to you, that the doctrine of the Trinity deprives him of all his fatherly attributes, and transfers them to the Son and the Holy Spirit? *Their* offices are all fatherly; *his* are those of the relentless potenate and judge. For which is the true Father,—he, who gives his life a ransom for the children; or he, who demands and receives the full price for their blood? Which is the true Father,—he, who sits cold and stern at the helm of the universe; or he, who draws nigh to the children's hearts in breathings of counsel, comfort, and hope? If this distinction between the three persons have any reality, is not he that redeems, or he that sanctifies, the Father? To which of these three persons does the Trinitarian come with the fullest assurance, in the most confiding manner, with the most trustful spirit? Not to the Father, (so called,) but to the Son. To the Father go up the cold and formal vows, the set praises; to the Son, the warm outpourings of the full heart, and those inward groanings, too deep, too fervent for utterance. Nor can it be rejoined, in answer to this reasoning, that the first person of the Trinity is called Father with reference to the other two persons, and not with reference to man. For the being, whom Jesus calls Father, he continually sets forth as man's Father. In talking to his disciples, he calls him *your* Father, as often as *my* Father; and even calls him by both titles in the same sentence, as, for instance, when he says: 'I ascend unto my Father, and your Father.' * Thus are the details

* John xx. 17.

of the doctrine of the Trinity at war with its phraseology. Does not this discrepancy indicate the error of man, rather than the wisdom of God? Would it not seem a mockery of human ignorance, for the Almighty to set forth his mere abstract essence, dread power, and infinite wisdom, and bid men call that cold abstraction *Father*, and to refuse this dearest of all names for those of his attributes, to which his children cling with filial confidence and love, — to make them cry, *Abba, Father*, where they feel not the spirit of the adoption, and to suppress that cry, where the heart is bursting to give it utterance? This must verily be the commandment of men, and not the doctrine of God.

But whence crept the Trinity into the Christian fold? This question I shall now answer by giving as brief a sketch as possible of the history of the Trinity. But the first part of my history must be that of simple Unitarianism; for vestiges of no other form of doctrine can be traced back farther than the third century, nor can we find any evidence that the doctrine of *three equal persons* in the Godhead was maintained till late in the fourth century. I am prepared to state, without fear of contradiction, that the doctrine of the *equality* of the Father, Son, and Holy Spirit, cannot be found in any work of the three first centuries, and that there cannot be found, with reference to the divine nature, in any genuine Christian work of the first two centuries, any statement of doctrine, equivalent, or approaching to, or consistent with, the modern doctrine of the Trinity. It is said, that, because there was no controversy about this doctrine, it was passed over in silence? I reply, that, as the Christian fathers wrote chiefly about the divine nature, attributes, and will, if they had this idea, they could not have failed to use corresponding phraseology; for Trinitarian phraseology is now used by Trinitarians, not only in controversial writings, but in prayers and in practical sermons, and has been freely used during ages when the doctrine was received without opposition or dissent.

Yet farther, it is as certain as any fact in history, that the Trinity was not in primitive times the doctrine of the whole Church, even if we were to admit that it was held by a part of the Church. No ecclesiastical historian denies or doubts that the Judaizing Christians of Palestine, who formed distinct sects early in the second century, were Unitarians. There were two sects of these Christians, — the Ebionites and the Nazarenes. The Ebionites believed Jesus to have been a mere man, the son of Joseph and Mary; and they are uniformly spoken of by the Orthodox fathers as heretics. The Nazarenes believed in the miraculous birth and superhuman dignity of Jesus, but regarded him as a created and finite being; and they seem to have been regarded as Orthodox in the earliest times, and are not spoken of as heretics till the fourth century. For these facts, it may be sufficient to refer you to the ecclesiastical history of Mosheim, himself a Trinitarian. Now could the Trinity have been believed by the great body of the Church during the first three centuries, and these Nazarenes have been left without anathema and obloquy?

There is yet another remark of importance to be made with regard to the early Christian writings. They consisted not only of works for the edification of those within the Church, but many of them were written for the defence and propagation of the new faith, and were addressed to Jews and Pagans, — to the opposers and persecutors of the Church. In writings of this class, the most important doctrine of the whole Christian system could not have been passed over in silence. It must needs have been clearly stated and expounded for the benefit of the uninitiated, and elaborately defended against doubts and objections. Let us see then what kind of language the early advocates of Christianity used in propagating and defending their religion.

On the day of Pentecost, Peter addressed a confused, skeptical, and mocking multitude, many of whom had come from afar, and were utter strangers to the new religion. Hear his simple statement, which made, we are told, *three thousand* converts: 'Jesus of Nazareth, a man approved of God among you, by miracles, and wonders, and signs, which God did by him in the midst of you, as ye yourselves also know; him, being delivered by the determinate counsel and foreknowledge of God, ye have taken, and by wicked hands have crucified and slain, whom God hath raised up.'* Hear also in what terms Paul preached Jesus for the first time before the superstitious and idolatrous Athenians: 'He hath appointed a day, in the which he will judge the world in righteousness, by that man whom he hath ordained, whereof he hath given assurance unto all men, in that he hath raised him from the dead.'† Hear also St. Paul's synopsis of his own preaching, in that bold, manly defence before Agrippa, in which you will all feel that it was infinitely beneath the apostle's character to have used concealment or equivocation: 'I continue unto this day, witnessing both to small and great, saying none other things than those which the prophets and Moses did say should come: that Christ should suffer, and that he should be the first that should rise from the dead, and should shew light unto the people, and to the Gentiles.'‡ *Saying none other things,'*— could St. Paul have honestly made such a denial

* Acts ii. 22–24. † Acts xvii. 31. ‡ Acts xxvi. 22, 23.

as this, if he had preached so novel and momentous a view of the divine nature as the Trinity unfolds, especially when it is considered that this must have been an entirely unknown doctrine to Agrippa?

The only other Christian apologist whom I have time to quote, is Justin Martyr, who addressed a defence of Christianity to Antoninus Pius about the year 140, and about the same time wrote a defence of Christianity against Jewish objections, in the form of a dialogue with Trypho the Jew. Justin, I remark in passing, has always held an unquestioned rank among the Orthodox fathers. Speaking of Jesus, (in the dialogue with Trypho,) he says: 'The Father is the author to him, both of his existence, and of his being powerful, and of his being Lord and divine.' 'He was subordinate to the Father, and a minister to his will.'

I will now offer you a few extracts from the fathers of the first three or four centuries, premising that I shall quote from no reputed heretic, but only from those, whom the Trinitarians regard as representatives of the Orthodoxy of their times. I shall have no difficulty, I think, in showing you that these fathers were what we now call Unitarians.

Clement of Rome, a personal friend of St. Paul, (believed on the concurring testimony of antiquity to be the Clement mentioned by St.

Paul in the epistle to the Philippians,)* styles Jesus 'the sceptre of the majesty of God.' We find, towards the close of his epistle to the Corinthians, the following doxology, — could a Trinitarian have written it? 'Now God, the Inspector of all things, the Father of all spirits, and the Lord of all flesh, who has chosen our Lord Jesus Christ, and us by him, to be his peculiar people, grant to every soul of man that calleth upon his glorious and holy name, faith, fear, peace, long-suffering, patience, temperance, holiness, and sobriety, unto all well-pleasing in his sight, through our High Priest and Protector, Christ Jesus, by whom be glory, and majesty, and power, and honor unto him, now and forever.'

Clement of Alexandria, who wrote near the beginning of the third century, says: 'The Mediator performs the will of the Father. The Word is the Mediator, being common to both, the Seal of God and the Saviour of men, God's Servant and our Instructor.'

Origen, the most learned of the fathers, wrote about the year 225. He says: 'The Father only is the Good; and the Saviour, as he is the image of the invisible God, so is he the image of his goodness.' 'If we know what prayer is, we must not pray to any created being, not to

* Philippians iv. 3.

Christ himself, but only to God, the Father of all, to whom our Saviour himself prayed.' 'We are not to pray to a brother, who has the same Father with ourselves, Jesus himself saying, that we must pray to the Father through the Son.' If this be not Unitarianism, what is it?

Eusebius, the father of ecclesiastical history, who wrote about the year 320, says: 'There is one God, and the only-begotten comes out of him.' 'Christ, being neither the Supreme God, nor an angel, is of a middle nature between them; and, being neither the Supreme God, nor a man, but the Mediator, is in the middle between them, the only-begotten Son of God.' 'Christ, the only-begotten Son of God, and the first-born of every creature, teaches us to call his Father the true God, and commands us to worship him only.'

I had marked for quotation many more extracts from the same and other fathers of the Church; but I omit them for the sake of brevity. And now let me ask, could these fathers have been Trinitarians, in the modern sense of that word? Could a modern Trinitarian have written the passages which I have now quoted? Had I quoted them, without naming their authors, would you not have taken them for extracts from the writings of Unitarian divines? I trust that there is no need of my saying, that I have endeavored to represent the opinions of those times impartially. During the second and third centuries, from a source which I shall shortly indicate, there was a gradual introduction of Trinitarian phraseology into the Church. But I no more believe that I myself am a Unitarian, than I do that the Christian fathers of the first three centuries, whose works have come down to us, were all of them virtually Unitarians. Though, from the time of Justin downward, there was a gradual departure from the simplicity of the gospel, and a tendency towards mystical views of the divine nature, and towards the recognition of a threefold distinction therein, yet I believe, that, down to the end of the second century at least, if not of the third, the doctrine of three equal persons in the Godhead would have been deemed as grossly heretical, as that of the undivided unity of God is anywhere regarded at the present time.

We have now reached the period of the Arian controversy, and the celebrated Council of Nice. The Arian controversy was on this wise. Alexander, bishop of Alexandria, in an assembly of his presbyters, maintained that the Son was of the same essence with the Father. This assertion was opposed by Arius, one of his presbyters, who maintained that the Son was totally and essentially distinct from the Father, being the first and noblest of his creatures. The dispute waxed warm, each side finding strong and determined champions, until at length Alexander summoned a numerous council, and deposed Arius and his adherents from their offices in the Church. Upon this, the controversy spread like wildfire, inflamed the whole church, and finally led to the summoning of the Council of Nice, which met in the year 325, condemned by vote of the majority the doctrine of Arius, procured his banishment into Illyria, and established what is called the Nicene Creed, — a creed not strictly Trinitarian, though strongly tending that way. This creed applied the title *God* to our Saviour; but calls him *God out of* or *derived from God*, and thus does not make him a self-existent and independent being, so that this last step towards the full development of the Trinity still remained to be taken. There was a large minority of the Council that dissented from this creed, though it was backed by the authority of the Emperor Constantine, who took an active part in the session. Only five years afterwards, the emperor, having become an Arian, repealed the laws against Arius, and instituted a series of oppressive measures against the partisans of the Nicene Creed. Ten years after the session of the Council of Nice, the Council of Tyre deposed Athanasius, Alexander's successor, and reinstated Arius and his adherents in their former offices and honors in the Alexandrian church. From this time, for a period of more than forty years, the Arian party generally had the supremacy; and the Nicene Creed could not, therefore, have been called the creed of the Church until near the close of the fourth century.

The Athanasian Creed is the oldest monument extant of the doctrine of three literally equal persons in the Godhead. This was probably written by Hilary, who died in the latter part of the fourth century. It has been recognized in the Romish Church as an authentic compend of faith, since the ninth or tenth century. It is retained in the English Book of Common Prayer; and its exclusion from the service of the American Episcopal Church was assented to with great reluctance by their transatlantic brethren. It is a very long and prolix document, and I cannot burden you with the whole of it; yet I am going to give you a pretty long extract from it, for two reasons, *first*, that you may see in its own canonical language what absurdities and contradictions the doctrine of the Trinity involves; and, *secondly*, that you may contrast it, as I read it, with the 'simplicity that is in Christ.'

'We worship one God in Trinity, and Trinity in Unity; neither confounding the persons, nor dividing the substance. For there is one person of the Father, another of the Son, and another of the Holy Spirit. But the Godhead of the Father, of the Son, and of the Holy Spirit is all one, the glory equal, the majesty co-eternal. Such as the

Father is, such is the Son, and such is the Holy Spirit. The Father uncreate, the Son uncreate, and the Holy Spirit uncreate. The Father incomprehensible, the Son incomprehensible, and the Holy Spirit incomprehensible. The Father eternal, the Son eternal, and the Holy Spirit eternal. And yet there are not three eternals, but one eternal. As also there are not three incomprehensibles, nor three uncreated; but one uncreate and one incomprehensible. So likewise, the Father is Almighty, the Son Almighty, and the Holy Spirit Almighty. And yet there are not three Almighties; but one Almighty. So the Father is God, the Son is God, and the Holy Spirit is God. And yet they are not three Gods, but one God. So likewise the Father is Lord, the Son Lord, and the Holy Spirit Lord; and yet not three Lords, but one Lord. For like as we are compelled by the Christian verity to acknowledge every person by himself to be God and Lord, so are we forbidden by the Catholic religion to say, There be three Gods or three Lords. . . . . And in this Trinity, none is fore or after other; none is greater or less than another; but the whole three persons are co-eternal together and co-equal.' Of all which and much more like it, the creed in its sequel charitably asserts, and the good people of the English Church are compelled by the rubric to hear on no less than *thirteen* Sundays and festivals in the year: 'Which faith except every one do keep whole and undefiled, without doubt he shall perish everlastingly.' The only appropriate response to this would be in the words of the apostles, 'Who then can be saved?'

We have now seen that the doctrine of the Trinity is not taught in the Bible, and that it formed no part of the Christian system as maintained by the primitive Church. Whence then came it? I have no hesitation in referring it to the Platonic philosophy. Plato had written much about three divine principles, which he had styled the One or the Good, Mind or Word, and Soul or Spirit. His followers had talked and written mystically about these same three principles, until the number *three* had become with them a sacred number, and a divine Trinity had assumed a prominent place among the doctrines of the later Platonists, insomuch that it may be traced in all their works. In process of time, many eminent Platonists became Christians. Justin Martyr was a devoted disciple of Plato. Alexandria, which, as we have seen, was the birth-place of the Christian Trinity, was the head-quarters of Platonism; and the early Trinitarian fathers were all Platonists, and were therefore Trinitarians before they became Christians. These fathers, having been much and long in the schools of philosophy, could not come to Jesus with the simplicity of little children. They were unwilling to be disciples of Christ alone. They quoted Plato and Jesus Christ in the same breath, believed in both with equally unhesitating assurance, incorporated the Platonic Trinity into their religious creed, remodelled the Christian system in the Platonic mould, and then complimented the memory of Plato on his having anticipated the essential doctrines of the gospel. That this statement is not exaggerated will appear from the fact, that, in their extant writings, the early Trinitarian fathers always quote Plato and his followers, as freely as they do the New Testament, on the subject of the Trinity. St. Augustine expressly says, that he was in the dark with regard to the Trinity, until he found the true doctrine concerning the divine Word in a Latin translation of some Platonic writings, which the providence of God had thrown in his way. I might, had I time, adduce numerous quotations from the Christian fathers to the same effect.

I have now accomplished, as far as possible within the limits of a single lecture, the work proposed. I have shown you, as I think, that the Trinity is not a doctrine of the Bible, that it was not believed or taught by the early Christian fathers, and that it derived a technical phraseology, its ideas and its ultimate form, from the Platonic philosophy.

One word in conclusion. If the view which I have now presented be just, ours is no new doctrine, but the faith first delivered to the saints. What we believe, was the creed of the Church in those days, when there were tongues of fire and hearts all zeal, when the word was quick and powerful, when the disciples offered their all upon the altar of their faith, and multitudes of such as should be saved were daily added to the company of the believers. Why may not the same creed bear like fruits now, and among us? May it not, God helping, if we are faithful to our light? Let us not, if we think that we have the truth, idly boast of our superior discernment; for it only makes our negligence and sluggishness the more blameworthy. Were we blind, we should have less sin. But now that we say, *We see*, our sin remains. If we have the light, let us walk as children of the light. If we deem ourselves, in our views of religious doctrine, more faithful than our fellow Christians to the sublime declaration of Moses, 'The Lord our God is one Lord,' let us be no less faithful to the commandment, which he annexes to that declaration, — 'Thou shalt love the Lord thy God with all thy heart, and with all thy soul, and with all thy might.'

LECTURE II.

JESUS CHRIST.

JOHN XIV. 28.

MY FATHER IS GREATER THAN I.

THE question of THE SUPREME DIVINITY OF JESUS CHRIST will be my subject this evening. I shall reserve for the next lecture, an explicit statement of my own views with reference to our Saviour's personal rank and character, and I shall now confine myself to the simple question: *Was Jesus of Nazareth identical with the Almighty Creator?*

Before entering upon my subject, suffer me to make one preliminary remark. There are two modes employed in proving doctrines from the Bible. One is the quotation of single texts, without reference to the context, or to the analogy of other portions of Scripture. The other is based upon the comparison of a text with its context, and of Scripture with Scripture; and has reference rather to the general tone and spirit of the sacred writings, or of particular books and passages, than to insulated words and phrases. The latter, I hardly need say, is the only true mode. By the former, any and every doctrine might be established; and its use has, in fact, led to most of the broad differences among Christians, and of the exceedingly wide departures from 'the simplicity that is in Christ.' No book in the world could bear such rules and modes of interpretation, as have been applied to the Bible. In all books, except scientific treatises, free use is made of metaphor and hyperbole, which are always defined and limited by what goes before and what follows, but which, taken by themselves and explained literally, would imply the most puerile and absurd notions. Now the fashion among theologians has been, to set up the seeming signification of some three or four isolated clauses in the Bible, as overweighing the clear and acknowledged tenor of the entire Scriptures, as if the inspired writers could have failed to recognize constantly, and to state explicitly, any fundamental doctrine of the religion, which they taught.

I can best illustrate the prevalent mode of Scriptural interpretation, by supposing a case. Suppose that, fifteen or twenty centuries hence, there should be remaining some two or three authentic biographies of Napoleon Bonaparte. Suppose that in one of these, written by an admiring Frenchman, it should be said of him:

'He was a very God among his soldiers, — adoring millions prostrated themselves before him, — he took in the nations of the earth at a glance, — his will was omnipotent.' Suppose that in another of these biographies, written by a bigoted English tory, it should be said of him: 'He was a very fiend incarnate, — the prince of darkness never let loose upon earth a more fearful angel of destruction.' Suppose that, though, elsewhere throughout these books, Napoleon was perpetually talked of as a man, and the books, taken as a whole, made utter nonsense upon the supposition that he was not a man, there yet should arise a set of critics, who maintained that Napoleon was a divine being, and another set, who maintained that he was a demon, — these two classes of critics would aptly represent the generality of modern theologians and biblical interpreters.

The true mode of interpretation obviously is, first, to get at the general tone and spirit of the book, or books, which we wish to interpret, and then, when we find a passage of difficult, doubtful, or ambiguous signification, to seek for it the interpretation, or to give it that one of several possible interpretations, which best accords with the tone and spirit of the whole. Thus, if the entire New Testament from beginning to end, if every discourse of our Saviour, if every exposition of Christian doctrine made by the apostles, if the whole tone of spiritual phraseology, declares, or necessarily implies, the inferiority of the Son to the Father, and yet there are some half-dozen or more, single texts, which seem to teach his supreme divinity, but admit of a different interpretation, I contend, that we are bound to interpret these texts in accordance with the voice of Scripture taken collectively; and I also maintain that, where there is any reasonable doubt with regard to the reading, or the punctuation of a passage, we are bound to prefer that reading, or that mode of punctuation, which best accords with the rest of the New Testament.

But let me not be misunderstood. I by no means say that half a dozen texts, or even a single text of Scripture, may not be sufficient to establish a religious doctrine. On the other hand, there are subjects spoken of but once or twice, on which I derive as definite and firm an opinion, from one or two texts, as I should from a volume. And if our Saviour were named but six times, or but once, in a series of books proffering the claims to plenary and conclusive authority, which, in my view, the New Testament proffers, and if, each of those six times, or that once, he were spoken of as the supreme God, I should then believe him to be the supreme God. But the case is very different. He speaks of himself, and is spoken of, many hundred times, in the New Testament. Take away some half-dozen, or, at most, a very few of these texts, and no one will contend that there remains a single case, in which the phraseology does not necessarily imply inferiority to the eternal Father. These few texts, as I interpret them, imply no other doctrine. But yet my Trinitarian brethren contend that they teach our Saviour's supreme divinity. Admitting, for the moment, that such were their most obvious meaning, the question is, whether they ought to outweigh the hundreds of texts that teach a different doctrine. Christ cannot be both a self-existent and a created being, both God and the Son of God, both equal and inferior to the Father. And if he, many hundreds of times, calls himself, and is called by his authorized interpreters, a created being, the Son of God, and inferior to the Father, then it seems to me that the few texts, which might bear a different meaning, ought to be interpreted in accordance with these hundreds of texts. With this general statement of facts in the case, I presume that no Trinitarian would find fault. But the Trinitarian would maintain that the hundreds of texts ought to be interpreted by the few.

These things premised, I now proceed to exhibit the chief reasons, why I find myself constrained to regard our Saviour as a created and subordinate being.

In the first place, our Saviour never declares

himself the supreme God, in any of the discourses or conversations recorded in the gospels. This is not a doctrine, for which it is common to appeal to our Saviour's own words; and yet, often as he spake of himself, and plain and confidential as was his intercourse with his disciples during the last scenes of his life, it hardly seems possible that he should have left them without a hint of his true nature and glory. I know of but two of his own sayings, which are ever quoted as referring to his supreme divinity; and I doubt whether these would be quoted in a serious argument. One of these is, 'I and my Father are one,'* which he sufficiently explains, when he afterwards prays for his disciples, 'that they may be one, even as we are one.'† The other is, 'He that hath seen me, hath seen the Father,'‡ which, in the next verse, he explains by saying: 'Believest thou not that I am in the Father, and the Father in me?' I am astonished that this should ever have been regarded as a Trinitarian proof-text. I know not a more decidedly anti-Trinitarian text in the Bible. For, if there be three distinct persons in the God-head, seeing one of them, is surely not seeing the other, — seeing the Father, is not seeing the Son. But if, as Unitarians believe, Christ dwelt in God, and God in him, if Christ was the image, the representative of the Father, then he, who

* John x. 30. † John xvii. 22. ‡ John xiv. 9.

had seen him, had seen the Father, — he, who had been conversant with the image, had become acquainted with the attributes of the original.

If our Saviour were indeed the supreme God, a fact, no less striking and unaccountable than his own silence on the subject, is, that the apostles did not proclaim him as God in their preaching to the unbelieving Jews and Gentiles. The cross, the ignominy, the lowly and suffering estate of Jesus, was the great stumbling-block to those, among whom they preached; and it was, therefore, a prime object with them to extol and exalt him, to set forth his claims upon the reverence of man, and to exhibit his intrinsic greatness and excellence. Was he, who was despised and rejected of men, indeed the Lord God Almighty? Of this fact, then, before all things else, would Peter have assured the unbelieving Jews, and Paul the inquisitive and credulous Athenians. This doctrine, so momentous, could not have been suppressed in preaching, to such a degree, as not once to find its way into the numerous discourses contained in the Acts of the Apostles. If Peter and Paul did not preach it, they cannot have believed it. If they did preach it, the eminently careful, faithful historian, St. Luke, could not have omitted this most prominent and striking point in their preaching.

I now offer you a consideration of very great,

and, it seems to me, decisive weight. If our Saviour were the almighty Creator, there was a time when his disciples first became aware of the fact; for they could not have believed it from the beginning. When Peter rebuked him, when they all forsook him, when they went weeping to his sepulchre, they could not have regarded him as God. Now, whenever they learned the fact of his supreme divinity, it must have wrought a marvellous and entire change in their feelings and conduct, — it must have created the most strongly marked epoch in the experience of their lives. It must have been with the utmost awe, with emotions of overpowering fulness that they ascertained that the Creator of all worlds had been dwelling with them, calling them his brethren, and submitting to their petulant and inconstant humors, — had broken bread for them, and even washed their feet. Must not such a stupendous discovery have left some trace of itself in the sacred record? Could it have taken place, without at least some notice of the time when, and the circumstances under which it was made? Did they first become aware of this fact after his resurrection? How then can we account for their preserving their former familiar, fraternal style of intercourse with him till the morning of the ascension? And yet their conversation with him that very morning, differs not in the least, as to its general tone and character, from those which they had held with him before his death. Or was it on the day of Pentecost that this amazing fact first became known to them? If so, would not Peter's discourse have been full of this new revelation? Could he have so entirely veiled the light that had just burst upon him, as coolly to commence his discourse: 'Jesus of Nazareth, a man approved of God among you, by miracles, and wonders, and signs, which God did by him,' and to utter not a single word, which the most astute critic can torture into a recognition of the deity of Christ? But it is impossible for the Trinitarian to say when the apostles were first apprised of this truth; nor is there, in the gospels or the Acts of the Apostles, the faintest trace of such a discovery having been made at any time. Now I could more easily account for the omission of all notice of our Saviour's birth, or death, or resurrection, or ascension, than for the omission or the announcement of this,— the most amazing and momentous fact of all,— indeed, the most interesting and important fact in the world's whole history.

I next remark that the whole phraseology of the New Testament, with regard to our Saviour, implies his created existence, and subordinate rank. In the first place, he is constantly called the *Son* of God. The word *Son*, as applied to him, either has, or has not, a meaning. If it has no meaning, then must it have been employed by our Saviour and his apostles in idle mockery of man's understanding, — a supposition unworthy to be entertained for a moment, and yet one, which our Trinitarian brethren cannot, it seems to me, entirely disavow. But if the word *Son* does mean anything, the least that it can imply is, that the Son owes his existence to the Father, therefore is not self-existent, did not then exist from all eternity, and consequently is not God.

I would next advert to the mode in which our Saviour uniformly speaks of himself. Here are some of his declarations, which I might multiply indefinitely: 'My Father is greater than I.'* 'I can of mine own self do nothing.'† 'The words that I speak unto you, I speak not of myself; but the Father that dwelleth in me, he doeth the works.'‡ 'I proceeded forth and came from God; neither came I of myself, but he sent me.'§ 'My meat is to do the will of him that sent me.'‖ 'Of that day and that hour knoweth no man, no, not the angels which are in Heaven, neither the Son, but the Father.'¶ 'God so loved the world, that he gave his only begotten Son.'** 'Why callest thou me good? there is none good but one, that is God.'†† 'I ascend

* John xiv. 28. † John v. 30. ‡ John xiv. 10.
§ John viii. 42. ‖ John iv. 34. ¶ Mark xiii. 32.
** John iii. 16. †† Matt. xix. 17.

unto my Father and your Father, and to my God and your God.'* But I might go on in this way, and quote from every chapter in the gospels, and from every verse in which our Saviour speaks, and show you every attribute of supreme divinity disclaimed, over and over again, from his own lips, without your being able to point to a single instance, in which he claims for himself any exclusively divine attribute. I might, also, show him to you praying to his Father, spending whole nights in supplication to Him, beseeching Him, if possible, to take from him the cup of death, and commending his departing spirit into the Father's hands.

It is said that Christ spoke and did thus in his human nature? To this I reply, in the first place, that the doctrine of the two natures of Christ is not claimed even by its advocates, as a doctrine of revelation. They quote no declaration, or passage of Scripture, in which they profess to find this doctrine expressed or implied. It is confessedly a hypothesis, which they have assumed, as the only mode in which they can reconcile Christ's supreme divinity with his own reiterated assertions to the contrary.

But this hypothesis of the two natures is far from obviating the difficulty, which it was designed to remove. If Christ be the supreme God, and if it be of any importance for man-

* John xx. 17.

kind to know the fact, it was of equal importance for him to have made the fact known, nor can there have been any adequate reason for his concealing it. Moreover, those, who maintain the doctrine of two natures, virtually charge our Saviour with equivocation. For does not the word *I* include the whole of the person speaking? I myself am composed of body and mind. I know that *five and five are ten.* My body does not know it; but my mind knows it. Now suppose that I should say, 'I do not know how much *five and five* are,' and should afterwards explain myself by saying, 'My body does not know it, and, when I spoke, I had reference to my body,' what would you think of my honesty, or good sense? You would certainly infer that I had made utter shipwreck of one or the other. Or suppose that I should say, 'I am unable to lift this manuscript,' and when you looked to see if I were smitten with a sudden paralysis, I should add, 'I only mean that my mind cannot lift it, — my body can,' you would surely regard my speech as anything but wise, and my intellect as anything but sane. Yet such is the imputation, which the doctrine of the two natures casts upon our Saviour; and his exalted mission, and the momentous subjects on which he spoke, only render the imputation the more gross and unworthy. If our Saviour was the supreme God, he knew the day and hour, which he said that he did not know, — he had himself the power to perform those works, which he said that he could not perform of himself, — he was the equal of the Father, whom he called greater than himself; and there remains no way, in which you can interpret these essentially false declarations from his lips, without casting reproach upon him, in whose pure and transparent spirit I believe that there was no guile. I press this point the more urgently, because to my eye the doctrine of our Saviour's supreme divinity renders all his recorded discourses a tissue of prevarication, fitted only to bewilder and mislead his hearers.

The hypothesis of the two natures also fails, inasmuch as Christ expressly disclaims the peculiar attributes of deity in some of those relations and offices, which it is contended that he fills by virtue of his divine nature. I know not how often I have seen and heard the number, variety, and magnitude of his miracles, and his sovereign sway over diseases and the elements, cited as demonstrative proof of his supreme divinity. But it is of these very miracles that he says: ' The works that I do, bear witness of me, that *the Father hath sent me*." * It is often said also, that none but God can be the final judge of man; and Christ's designated office as judge of the living and the dead is referred to in every de-

* John v. 36.

fence of the Trinity, as proof positive of his supreme divinity. But of this office he says: '*The Father hath committed* all judgment unto the Son;' and, a few sentences afterwards, assigns not his deity, nor even his close connection with the Father, but, on the other hand, his relationship to man, as the reason why he is appointed man's judge: 'He hath given him authority to execute judgment also, *because he is the Son of man.*' *

We have then our Saviour's uniform and often repeated testimony to his own created existence and subordinate rank, in maintaining which we cannot surely be guilty of denying the Lord Jesus, inasmuch as we fasten our faith upon his own words.

Do we look to the rest of the New Testament? We still find our Saviour spoken of as a created and subordinate being. 'Him hath God ordained,'—'Him hath God raised up,'—'Him hath God set forth,'—is the burden of the apostolic preaching. How many times do the apostles designate the Almighty as the *God*, or the *Father of our Lord Jesus Christ!* Says St. Paul: 'There is one God, and one mediator between God and men, the man Christ Jesus.' † And again: 'Ye are Christ's, and Christ is God's.' ‡ Says St. John: 'God loved us, and sent his Son to be the propitiation for our sins;'

* John v. 22, 27. † 1 Tim. ii. 5. ‡ 1 Cor. iii. 23.

and again, in the same chapter: 'The Father sent the Son to be the Saviour of the world.'* The apostles speak also of Christ, in his glorified state, as making intercession for his Church. 'Who also maketh intercession for us.'† 'If any man sin, we have an advocate with the Father, Jesus Christ the righteous.'‡ If Christ be God, to whom does he pray?

The apostles speak of Christ as subordinate to the Father, even in those passages, in which they ascribe to him the highest exaltation and glory; nay, in the very passages, which are currently quoted in proof of his supreme divinity on the alleged ground, that such honor can be rendered to no created being. Take this passage for instance: 'Wherefore God also hath highly exalted him, and given him a name which is above every name, that at the name of Jesus every knee should bow, of things in heaven, and things in earth, and that every tongue should confess that Jesus Christ is Lord, to the glory of God the Father.'§ *God hath exalted him,* — *God hath given him a name,* — *to the glory of God the Father.* How could his derived and subordinate nature have been more strongly expressed?

There is a passage in one of St. Paul's epistles

* 1 John iv. 10, 14. † Rom. viii. 34.
‡ 1 John ii. 1. § Phil. ii. 9, 11.

to the Corinthians, where the extent and universality of Christ's reign are spoken of in more ample and lofty terms than anywhere else in the New Testament; but, as if to preclude the inference of his independent and supreme divinity, the apostle adds: 'When all things shall be subdued unto him, then shall the Son also himself be subject unto him that put all things under him, that God may be all in all.'*

I might also quote that passage in the Epistle to the Hebrews, where God is represented as saying to Christ, in language borrowed from the Old Testament, (in which a more free use is made of the word *God*, than in the New,) 'Thy throne, O God, is forever and ever;' but it is added, 'God, even *thy God*, hath anointed thee with the oil of gladness above thy fellows,' † — a passage, which suggests the inquiry, — If Christ was the supreme God, who was his God, who were his fellows, and who anointed him? And throughout the introduction of this epistle, in which it seems the writer's sole object to heap the praises of a pious and grateful heart upon the glorified Redeemer, we have multiplied recognitions of his subordinate rank with reference to the Father. 'Whom he *hath appointed* heir of all things, *by whom* also he made the worlds.' ‡ 'It became him, for whom are all

* 1 Cor. xv. 24–28. † Heb. i. 8, 9. ‡ Heb. i. 2.

things, and by whom are all things, in bringing many sons unto glory, *to make the captain of their salvation perfect through sufferings;* for both he that sanctifieth, and they that are sanctified, *are all of one:* for which cause he is not ashamed to call them *brethren;* saying, I will declare thy name unto *my brethren:* in the midst of the church *will I sing praise unto thee.* And again, *I will put my trust in him.* And again, Behold I and the children which *God hath given me.* . . . . . *In all things* it behoved him to be made *like unto his brethren.* . . . . In that he himself hath suffered, *being tempted*, he is able to succor them that are tempted.'* Now all these things may be said of the most highly exalted of God's children; but surely not of God himself. Men are not God's brethren. God cannot sing praise to himself. God cannot be tempted; nor can he have been made perfect through suffering.

In the Epistle to the Colossians, where it is said of Christ, that 'by him were all things created that are in heaven, and that are in earth,' and that 'he is before all things,' he is in the same sentence styled, not the Uncreated, but 'the first-born of every creature,' therefore not self-existent, and consequently not God.†

In the Apocalypse, where the highest titles

* Heb. ii. 10–18. † Col. i. 15–17.

and honors are given to our Saviour, and where the rapt apostle sees the ransomed hosts casting down their crowns before him, he is still represented as a created being. Though he styles himself 'Alpha and Omega, the first and the last,'* he still indicates that these expressions denote not the uncreated source of being, but the first-born Son; for he afterwards calls himself '*the beginning of the creation of God.*'† And again, while the redeemed are represented as assigning for the reason of their praise to the Father: 'Thou hast created all things, and for thy pleasure they are and were created;'‡ to the Son their words are: 'Thou *wast slain*, and hast redeemed us *unto God* by thy blood, out of every kindred, and tongue, and people, and nation, and hast made us *unto our God*, kings and priests,'§ — an ascription, of which every candid mind must see at once that the supreme God cannot be the subject.

I next remark, that Christ did not present himself as an object of adoration, and that he commanded his disciples to offer prayer, not to himself, but to his Father. I know not what could be more explicit than the following passage, where, speaking of the time when he should no longer be with his disciples, he says to them: 'In that day ye shall ask me nothing.

* Rev. i. 11. † Rev. iii. 14.
‡ Rev. iv. 11. § Rev. v. 9, 10.

Verily, verily, I say unto you, whatsoever ye shall ask the Father in my name, he will give it you.' *

In accordance with these words of their Master, all the recorded prayers of the apostles are directed to God, generally through Christ, or in his name; nor do they, in a single instance, exhort their convert to pray or to give thanks to Jesus, but to God the Father, in the name of the Lord Jesus Christ. The only case, I believe, in which authority for prayer to Christ is drawn from the New Testament, is that of the dying Stephen, when he said, 'Lord Jesus, receive my spirit.' † But this was not prayer. This was not an address to an invisible being. It was speaking to one whom he saw. The heavens were opened, and he saw 'Jesus standing on the right hand of God.' He had a vision of the risen Saviour, with a countenance and gesture of welcome for his dying servant. He thus commended his spirit to one, who had personally appeared, to lead him through the dark valley to the mansion of eternal rest.

One word more concerning this text. In our common Bible, it reads: 'They stoned Stephen, calling upon *God*, and saying, Lord Jesus, receive my spirit.' But you will see that the word *God* is printed in italics. In this type are printed

* John xvi. 23. † Acts vii. 59.

those words in the translation, which have no corresponding words in the original, but which the translators saw fit to supply. There are many, I suppose, who do not know what the italics in the Bible mean; and the explanation of them ought to be printed in every copy. This text, omitting the word inserted by the translators, would read: 'They stoned Stephen, calling upon, or invoking, (of course the person last named, and that is Jesus,) and saying, Lord Jesus, receive my spirit.' There is another instance, in which our translators have inserted the same word *God*. It is this: 'Hereby perceive we the love *of God*, because he laid down his life for us.' * The words *of God*, are in italics, and have nothing corresponding to them in the original, which, literally rendered, reads: 'Hereby perceive we love, because he laid down his life for us.'

But, to return from this digression, there is not, in the New Testament a single instance of prayer to Jesus, nor is there a single case, in which homage is paid to him in the way in which it is paid to God. There are indeed many ascriptions of praise to him; but they are always accompanied with the specific designation of his work and office as Mediator, and generally with an express reference to the eternal Father as

* John iii. 16.

alone supreme. But there are several instances, in which persons are said to have *worshipped* Jesus. The word translated *worship*, however, does not necessarily denote the rendering of divine honors, but simply prostration, or other external marks of homage or reverence, such as are paid by inferiors to superiors, by subjects to princes, and by servants to masters. For instance, the servant in the parable, who owed a thousand talents, fell down at his master's feet, 'and *worshipped* him, saying, Lord, have patience with me, and I will pay thee all.'* Indeed, most of these cases of *worship* or prostration before our Saviour, were cases of suppliants asking favors of him, at a time when, it is generally contended by Trinitarians, our Saviour's supreme divinity had not yet been made known.

Such is the state of facts with reference to the recognition of our Saviour's supreme divinity by the apostles, in appropriate acts of devotion. Now, that neither prayer nor divine honors should have been rendered to our Saviour by his apostles seems to me entirely unaccountable, if he were properly the subject of them. It is equally unaccountable, that, if they had been rendered, no instance of the kind should have remained on record in the New Testament. And still more strange is it, that, if Jesus be the

* Matthew xviii. 26.

supreme God, he himself should not only have omitted to enjoin, but should have expressly forbidden prayer to himself, and should have prescribed a mode of prayer, in which he was indeed to be recognized as the Mediator, but not as the object of prayer.

I will now ask your attention to some of the single texts urged by those who maintain the supreme deity of Christ. I do not intend (for I have not time) to bring forward all the proof-texts that have been urged or relied upon. But I shall choose those, which seem to me the strongest, and those on which eminent Trinitarians have laid the most stress. I shall purposely omit only those, on which no independent reliance is placed, but which are brought forward as subsidiary to the argument based upon the others. And let me add, that, should I omit in this lecture the consideration of texts, which any of you desire to hear discussed, if you will name such texts to me, they shall be taken up in the next lecture.

Those, who maintain the supreme divinity of our Saviour, rest for this doctrine, if I am not mistaken, solely on single texts. They draw no argument from the general tone and spirit of the New Testament. They admit that the argument from this source, so far as it has any bearing, goes against them. But they deem it overborne by the clearness and weight of the single texts, which they quote in behalf of their dogma.

Of these texts, I set aside, as having no bearing on the doctrine in question, those, which simply teach our Saviour's continued presence with his Church, and his power over the spiritual creation of God; for these are truths of which I entertain not the slightest doubt; they imply no more than a headship over the Church, conferred by the Father, and are but the fulfilment of those words of our Saviour: 'All power *is given* unto me in heaven and in earth.'* *Is given*, — given then by the Being, to whom it of right belonged, and who is as competent to constitute the ascended Redeemer head of the whole spiritual family above and below, as to make you and me fathers and heads of our own little households. Nor need we here consider those texts which imply, or seem to imply, our Saviour's preëxistence; for the question, whether he existed before his birth in Bethlehem, is entirely independent of that of his supreme divinity.

The only text from the Old Testament, much relied on by the advocates of the doctrine in question, is this from Isaiah: 'Unto us a child is born, unto us a son is given: and the government shall be upon his shoulder: and his name shall be called Wonderful, Counsellor, *the mighty*

* Matthew xxvii. 18.

God, the everlasting Father, the Prince of Peace.'* In this text, the Hebrew word rendered *God*, is not *Elohim*, the word commonly so rendered; but *El*, of which *God* is only a secondary meaning. The Hebrew Lexicons give for its meaning, *first*, (as an adjective,) *strong*, *mighty; secondly*, (as an abstract noun,) *strength*, *power;* and *thirdly* and often, (by a natural transfer from an abstract to a concrete sense,) *God*. Our translators chose the *last* of the *three* meanings. I am disposed to think the *first* the true signification here, and should render the passage: 'He shall be called Wonderful, Counsellor, Strong, Mighty, Father of eternity, that is, Author of eternal life, (or, perhaps, Father or Author of an age,—a new age or dispensation,) Prince of Peace.'

Another text much relied on is from the Epistle to the Philippians: 'Let this mind be in you, which was also in Christ Jesus, who, being in the form of God, *thought it not robbery to be equal with God;* but made himself of no reputation, and took upon him the form of a servant.' † The true sense of this passage, according to many *Trinitarian* commentators, is this: 'Let the same mind be in you, which was also in Christ Jesus, who, though in the form, the image of God, yet *did not covet to appear as God*, that

* Isaiah ix. 6.

† Philippians ii. 5–7.

is, did not exalt or magnify himself; but, on the other hand, humbled himself; and took upon him the form of a servant.' But, however this passage may be interpreted, any possible inference from it in favor of the supreme divinity of Christ is negatived by the sequel of the sentence, in which the apostle says that, on account of his thus humbling himself, '*God has highly exalted him*, and *has given* him a name above every name, that at the name of Jesus every knee should bow, ... *to the glory of God the Father.*'

Another important text is this from the Epistle to the Romans: 'Whose are the fathers, and of whom, as concerning the flesh, Christ came, who is over all, *God blessed forever*. Amen.'* The New Testament, like all books of that age, was originally written without stops, and without division of sentences. The stops have been inserted, and the sentences divided in comparatively recent times. I suppose, in common with many very eminent biblical critics, that, in this passage, there should be a full stop after the words, *over all;* and that the words, 'God blessed forever, — Amen,' were added as a doxology by the apostle, in the way, in which, in several instances, he has inserted a doxology in the midst of a paragraph.

* Romans ix. 5.

The exclamation of Thomas, when he recognized his risen Master, '*My Lord and my God*,'* is quoted as a proof-text for the doctrine under discussion, though I am surprised that it should be. It was a mere exclamation of glad astonishment on the part of Thomas. It was not addressed to Christ; for it is not in the vocative case, which is used in the Greek when a person is spoken to. The words *Lord* and *God* are both in the nominative case. The sentence is elliptical; and, were we to supply the ellipsis, it would, as I suppose, read thus: 'It is my Lord and my God, that has brought this glorious event to pass.' But it was an abrupt, fragmentary exclamation, such as would naturally spring from overwhelming surprise, — not profane, because uttered in deep solemnity and awe, and in clear recognition of the divine hand, which had raised his Master from the dead. It was the most natural of all exclamations under the circumstances in which it was uttered. Suppose that some one, whom we knew to have been long dead, should stand forth here in the presence of us all, would not the exclamation, *My God*, be the solemn, fervent, heart-stricken utterance of every one present? That any argument should ever have been based upon this exclamation seems to me excessively strange, when I con-

* John xx. 28.

sider the whole connection in which it stands. Thomas had, a moment before, expressed his entire unbelief as to the identity of his Master. Jesus then showed him his wounds, to convince him of his identity. This was all that he undertook to prove to Thomas, and all that the wounds could prove. Now, if Thomas had ever believed Christ to be God, he would never have doubted his power to rise from the dead. His skepticism with regard to the resurrection, proves that he had not previously believed that Christ was God. But Christ's resurrection no more proved him to be God, than the rising of Lazarus proved him to be God. Thomas had therefore had no proof of his Master's supreme divinity presented to his mind; and one, so slow to believe as he was, could hardly have leaped to so momentous a conclusion, without something on which to base it.

The next passage, to which I shall refer, is this from the first Epistle to Timothy: "Without controversy, great is the mystery of godliness: *God was manifest in the flesh, justified in the spirit, seen of angels, preached unto the Gentiles, believed on in the world, received into glory.*'* There is much discrepancy with regard to the reading of this passage among the early manuscripts and versions; but, to my mind, the

* 1 Timothy iii. 16.

balance of argument is in favor of the common reading, and the text conveys to my apprehension, nothing, which I do not gladly believe and embrace. Nay, I would adopt the passage as embodying my confession of faith with regard to Jesus Christ. I joyfully and thankfully acknowledge, that, in the person, in the moral attributes, in the unquenchable love of Jesus, God *was manifest in the flesh*,—that he was *justified*, that is, had false notions and sentiments concerning himself uprooted, and true ideas and feelings implanted among men, *through* the workings of *his spirit*,—that *angels beheld* with adoration this display of divine wisdom and love,—that God thus manifested was *proclaimed to the Gentiles*,—*believed on in the world*,—*received in glory*, (for such is the literal rendering of the words,) that is, gloriously received and welcomed in the hearts of Christ's true disciples.

In the Acts of the Apostles, St. Paul bids the Ephesian elders to 'feed the church *of God*, which he hath purchased *with his own blood*.'* *Lord* occurs here instead of *God* in many of the earlier manuscripts and versions, and is deemed the true reading by the best critics. But I will take the text as it stands, and will seek no advantage from the difference of reading. Now, were it the general voice of the New Testament

* Acts xx. 28.

that the supreme God suffered, and died, and shed his blood upon the cross, I should certainly interpret this text as referring to his death. But, the contrary being the voice of the New Testament, if I admit the common reading of this passage, I must interpret it in accordance with what I know St. Paul to have believed and taught. Now St. Paul uniformly taught that 'God spared not his own Son, but delivered him up for us all;' and I must, therefore, suppose *blood*, in the passage under discussion, to denote *Son*, as it does, in common with the word *flesh*, in all languages, both ancient and modern. 'He hath purchased with his own *blood*,' that is, with his own *Son*.

I now ask your attention, for a few moments, to the introduction of St. John's gospel. In order to understand this, we must look at the purpose for which St. John wrote his gospel. On this subject, we are fortunate in having, among others, a competent and unimpeachable witness in Irenæus,—a friend and pupil of Polycarp, who was a personal friend of St. John. It is the uniform testimony of antiquity, that St. John wrote his gospel after the other *three*, and at Ephesus,—the head-quarters of the Gnostic heresy, which was the first wide departure from the simplicity of the Christian faith; and Irenæus says, that the beloved disciple wrote his gospel for the express purpose of refuting the false and absurd notions, which the Gnostics were beginning to spread in Asia Minor. It concerns us then to know what the Gnostics believed. They engrafted upon the Christian faith a hybrid philosophy, or to speak more correctly, they engrafted some few Christian phrases and ideas upon a hybrid philosophy, in which Platonism was blended with the oriental mysticism. They maintained that the supreme God dwelt in the remote heavens, surrounded by chosen spirits, *Æons*, (as they called them,) and gave himself very little concern with what took place upon earth; that the world was created by an inferior and imperfect being, who was also the author of the Jewish dispensation; that Christ was sent by the supreme God to deliver men from the tyranny of this creator, and from the yoke of his law; that there were also various created spirits, or *Æons*, sustaining different offices, independently for the most part of the supreme Deity, the names of some of which *Æons* were *Life*, *Light*, and particularly, the *Logos* or *Word*, which represented the divine *Reason* or *Wisdom;* and that the *Æon Light* became incarnate in John the Baptist. All these spiritual existences were represented as distinct from each other, and from the supreme God, so that the system was a sublimated form of polytheism. To fuse these disjointed fragments of deity into one, — to rebuke these babblings of philosophy, falsely so called, about a divided sceptre and a scattered divinity, — this was the purpose of St. John's introduction. And not only so; but we find that the same pervading purpose gives shape, and character, and, as it were, the key-note, to his whole gospel. With this object in view, it was incumbent on him to show that *Life*, and *Light*, and the *Logos* or *Word*, were not distinct from the supreme God; that the supreme God created the world, and gave the Jewish law; that the same God sent John, the forerunner; and that the same God sent Jesus Christ, not to destroy, but to complete the law, — not to deliver men from its tyranny, but to finish for them the work, which the law had begun. And this is shown in the first *eighteen* verses of the gospel, — how comprehensively and beautifully you will see, if you keep in mind what I have told you of the Gnostic notion, while I read the passage to you, with such explanations that may be requisite.

In the beginning was the Word, the Logos, the divine Reason or Wisdom, — not a created being, nor yet an emanation from the Supreme; but it always existed, — *the Word was with God*, and never had a separate existence; *and the Word was God*, was and is inseparable from his essence and his attributes. *The same* Word, the same divine Wisdom, repeats the evangelist, *was in the beginning with God.* And now St. John directs his attention to another of the Gnostic errors, namely, that of the world's having been created by an inferior divinity. *All things*, says St. John, *were made by him*, that is, by God, (not by the Word,—*him* refers to *God*, which is the nearest preceding noun to which it can refer.) All things were made by the supreme God, *and without him was not anything made that was made. In him also was Life; and the Life was the Light of men.* Life and Light are not distinct essences; but God is the source of life, and, where it flows from him, light flows with it. *And the Light shines in darkness; but the darkness comprehended it not.* God has shed light upon men in the darkest times, though men have chosen darkness rather than light.

There was a man sent from God whose name was John. He came for a witness, to bear testimony of the light, concerning the divine light, *that all men through him might believe. He was not that light*, not himself an Æon, a spiritual emanation,—he was a man, like other men; *but was sent to bear witness of the Light.* He, from whom he came, *God*, *was the true Light that enlightens every man that comes into the world.* God had not removed himself from his creation, had not dwelt apart in the remote heavens. *He was* already, he was always *in the world, and the world had been made by him; yet the world knew him not. He had come to his own*, to the Jewish nation, his favored and covenant people; *but his own received him not;* that is, as a nation, they had in general disowned and rejected him in heart and deed, though not in name. *But to as many as received him*, to the patriarchs and to the faithful among their posterity, *to them who believed on his name, he gave power to become the sons of God*, his own spiritual children, *born, not of blood, nor of the will of the flesh, nor of the will of man*, (children not in any human or earthly sense,) *but of God.*

And, in these latter days, *the Word*, the divine Wisdom, *became flesh, and dwelt among men; and we*, I and my fellow apostles, *beheld its glory,—the glory of the only begotten*, of the chosen Son, *of the Father, full of mercy and of truth.*

John bore testimony concerning him, and cried, saying, This is he, of whom I said, He that cometh after me, has taken precedence of me; for he was before me,—was my superior. *And of his fulness*, of the rich truth and mercy of the Word made flesh, *have we all received;* yet not, as false teachers now say, mercy instead of wrath, a silken instead of an iron yoke, but *grace for grace*,—one gracious dispensation to supersede another. *For the law was given through Moses*, and that was a law of mercy, adapted to its own times; *but* now *mercy and truth* for all times *have come through Jesus Christ. No man has seen*

God at any time; the only begotten Son, who is in the bosom of the Father, he has declared him, has made him known.

Thus we see that the introduction of John's gospel, so far from authorizing the breaking up of the divine nature into a plurality of persons, is a noble assertion and vindication of the divine unity, well worthy the pen of inspiration, — a passage, in which, as with a prophet's wand, he waves back to their native nothingness the chimeras of an arrogant and impious philosophy.

But I have spoken long enough, perhaps too long. I have shown you, as I trust, that the general tenor of the New Testament, and numberless express declarations of our Saviour and his apostles, oblige us to regard him, though second only to the Father, as holding with reference to the Father a derived existence, and a subordinate rank. I have heaped up an amount of testimony, which much more than convinces me, — which leaves my own mind, I can truly say, without the shadow of a doubt, — with a conviction, which has no room to grow stronger. I have also, I think, selected all the really strong and difficult texts alleged in proof of the opposite doctrine. Some of them, I confess, would have weight, were they not overborne by such an overwhelming amount of testimony on the other side. But not one of them requires, and some of them do not in my view admit, the interpretation, which favors the supreme divinity of Christ.

I now commend the subject to your own serious reflection and study. But, while you seek and prize just ideas of your Saviour's rank and character, remember that your truest knowledge of him, is heart-knowledge,—that knowledge, which you can have only by being like him,—by following him,—by having 'Christ in you, the hope of glory.'

LECTURE III.

JESUS CHRIST.

MATTHEW XXII. 42.

WHAT THINK YE OF CHRIST?

My two previous lectures have been devoted to the defence of the divine unity, in opposition to the unscriptural doctrines of the Trinity, and the supreme deity of Christ. The present lecture will be devoted to the explanation of my own views of THE NATURE AND CHARACTER OF CHRIST, with this reservation, that I shall omit all considerations bearing directly upon the *atonement*, which I shall make the subject of two distinct lectures at the close of the course.

In the first place, I pretend not that the difference between our Trinitarian brethren and ourselves, as to the person of our Saviour, is a slight one. I regard it indeed as not fundamental; for we all alike look to God as the author of our pardon and our eternal life,— they supposing that God brought these blessings into the world in his own person,— we, that he bestowed them through the hand of a Mediator. But, however high the personal rank which we assign to our Saviour, there is an infinite distance between God and the loftiest of created and finite beings; and our Saviour, if created and finite, was a son of God, and a brother of man, — titles, which he assumes, and uses freely with regard to himself, but which he could not have employed, had he been the supreme God.

But while I deny the personal deity of Christ, I most firmly believe in his *divinity*, — in a divinity, created by a constant and full indwelling and inworking of the Father in the Son. He was, in the highest possible degree, the sanctified, the empowered, the sent, the vicegerent, the representative of God.

The Scriptures place him before us under two leading aspects, (which resolve themselves into one,) as *the perfect image of God, and the perfect pattern of human virtue.*

First, as the *perfect image of God.* This is indicated in many passages of Scripture, as, for instance, in the following: 'Being the brightness of God's glory, and the express image of his person.'* 'In him dwelleth all the fulness of the Godhead bodily.'† 'He that hath seen me, hath seen the Father.'‡ 'The Word was made flesh, and dwelt among us.'§ In the introduc-

* Hebrews i. 3.
† Colossians ii. 9.
‡ John xiv. 9.
§ John i. 14.

tion of St. John's gospel, from which this last text is quoted, we have, it seems to me, the whole theory of our Saviour's relation to God. There we are told, that the Word, the divine Reason or Wisdom, — the same divine attributes, which had been manifested in creation and in the whole course of providence, — assumed a human form, and dwelt among men in the person of Jesus of Nazareth. We are also told in the same connection, why this manifestation of the Deity took place. 'God was in the world, and the world was made by him, and the world knew him not.' His power and his love were enshrined in all the forms, and uttered themselves in all the voices of outward nature, — the heavens and the earth were full of them; but they were diffused over too wide a surface, for man anywhere to take in a clear and satisfying view of them. Man saw the rays of divinity; but could not trace them to their source. The attributes of God were in the universe, as we may suppose light to have been before the sun was made, spread everywhere, but concentrated nowhere. But, as God placed in the centre of our system a vast urn, to which men should look as the prime source of light, and brought together there, and caused to stream from thence, the rays, which before had mingled, and crossed each other from every point of the horizon, — so, in the moral firmament, did he kindle Jesus as the sun of righteousness, and combined and concentrated in his person rays of divinity, which, though shed all over creation, had never been brought together on earth before. We see in Jesus as much of God as can be made manifest in a created being, — the fulness of the Godhead in the flesh, — the outermost limit of the finite, — the nearest approach to the infinite.

But here there is an obvious distinction to be made between God's *physical* and his *moral* attributes. By the *physical*, we denote *power* and *wisdom*, to which alone the word *infinite* can be applied with precision. These, of course, cannot belong in their entire fulness to any subordinate being; for, if any being possessed them, the possession of them would make him God. Our Saviour expressly disclaims them, when he says, 'I can of mine own self do nothing,' and when he speaks of himself as ignorant of the day and hour, which the Father knew. The highest possible power and wisdom of a created being must needs be finite, and must therefore fall infinitely short of those attributes as they exist in God. Yet of these attributes, of the divine omnipotence and omniscience, our Saviour bore the express image. He wrought the works, and uttered the words of God. He took the things of God, and showed them to men. His miracles manifested divine power in every department of nature. The sea obeyed him; and the winds were still at his voice. Water blushed to wine; and bread in the desert grew beneath his touch. He poured light upon the sightless balls, and the tide of health through the palsied limbs. The lame leaped in gladness before him; and the dumb broke forth in hosannas to the Son of David. He raised the dying from the death-bed, — the dead from their bier and the tomb. He thus laid bare the arm of omnipotence, revealed the hidings of divine power, — wrought, without any intermediate agency, such works as, through second causes, through the common processes of nature, are wrought at all times by the Almighty. By these marvellous works, Christ represents to our hearts, and brings home to our faith, the divine omnipotence. His miracles gave us a consciousness of repose on an Almighty arm. When we contemplate what he wrought, we feel more than ever that the universe is not its own, but our Father's, — that its giant forces are balanced and governed by him, who numbers the very hairs of our heads. These mighty works rebuke our despondency, and give us a calm trust in that Providence, which does all things well.

Christ also comes to us as the image of the divine omniscience. He brings to us, from the infinite treasury of wisdom and knowledge, all that we need to know. He gives us assurance under the seal of God, wherever we might remain in doubt. He speaks with authority, — declares to us what he has seen with God, — brings us revelations from the bosom of the Father. His teachings are not inferences from trains of argument; but portions of absolute, eternal truth, — transcripts from the infinite mind.

With regard to the *moral* attributes of God, — his *justice*, *holiness*, and *love*, — *perfection*, not *infinity*, is the word which characterizes them; and, in these attributes, a finite being may be perfect, even as God is perfect; that is, may, in his sphere of knowledge, power, and duty, manifest, without deviating from them, the same attributes which God manifests throughout the universe, — may be, in his limited range and capacity, no less good, just, and holy, than God is. But we are acquainted with no perfect child of God, except our Saviour. Of him alone is the testimony borne: 'He did no sin.' He 'is holy, harmless, undefiled.' He 'was in all points tempted like as we are, yet without sin.' He alone, of all that have dwelt upon earth, could say with literal and unexaggerated truth, 'Father, I have finished the work which thou gavest me to do.' We feel, as we read the gospel, that we are communing with spotless and divine perfection. We see there a virtue, beyond which no dreams of perfection can reach, — a transparent purity, in which the carping infidel can detect no shadow of dimness, — a love unlimited and inexhaustible. And, when we hear him say, 'He that hath seen me, hath seen the Father,' we rejoice to know that the amiable and inviting traits, which temper the majesty of the Saviour's character, belong to the Father that sent him. When we view the Father through the Son, we ascribe to him with confidence all the most tender and attractive forms of love, with which we are conversant, such as meekness and forbearance, pity and compassion, tender watchfulness and care over the minutest objects and concerns. The life of Jesus, considered as the image of God, gives a new and heart-reaching emphasis to the declarations of holy writ: 'As a father pitieth his children, so the Lord pitieth them that fear him; for he knoweth our frame; he remembereth that we are dust;' — 'a father of the fatherless, and a judge of the widows, is God in his holy habitation;' — 'He provideth for the raven his food, — his young cry unto God.'

There is nothing mystical in the aspect of our Saviour's character, which I have now presented. It only supposes that, which takes place partially in every good man, to have taken place in Jesus to an unlimited and perfect degree. God manifests himself in every wise and holy man. Whenever we do God's will, he dwells and works in us. But that spirit, which in us is shed abroad so imperfectly, and is so often quenched by doubt, folly, and sin, was on Jesus shed without measure, pervaded every faculty of his soul, prompted his every word and deed; in fine, constituted his only principle of life and of energy. Indeed, all moral goodness is the same in kind, — it differs only in degree.

This leads me next to speak of Jesus as *the perfect pattern for man* in all the duties of a creature and a fellow-creature, — of a child and a brother. He bears the divine image, that we may bear it also, — that we, beholding with open countenance the glory of God in the face of Jesus, may be changed into the same image, — that, in St. Peter's language, we may 'be partakers of the divine nature,' and, in St. Paul's, may 'be followers of God as dear children.' Through the imitation of Jesus, is one and the same moral image to be reflected by all true children of God. They are to purify themselves as he is pure. When he shall appear, they are to be like him; and thus, in every disciple, are the words of his prayer to be fulfilled: 'The glory which thou gavest me, I have given them, that they may be one, even as we are one, I in them, and thou in me.'

I have thus presented our Saviour under the two prominent aspects, in which, it seems to me, the Scriptures present him, as God's image and man's exemplar. In these aspects, I am accustomed to think of him as abiding still and forever, to his disciples. As on earth, so now in heaven, do the ransomed hosts behold him as 'the brightness of the Father's glory;' and there, as here, is it their privilege to 'follow the Lamb whithersoever he goeth.' The New Testament always speaks of the life of the redeemeed in heaven, as in close personal connection with Jesus. He appears to the dying Stephen, and receives his ascending spirit. St. Paul speaks of his desire to depart, and to be with Christ.' St. John says of those, 'which came out of great tribulation,' that 'the Lamb which is in the midst of the throne shall feed them, and shall lead them unto living fountains of waters.' Finite spirits, even through a boundless eternity, can never, 'by searching find out the Almighty unto perfection;' and the idea seems to me consonant with both reason and Scripture, and meets with a grateful response from the heart that truly loves Jesus, that he will through eternity be our guide to the more perfect knowledge of God, and our forerunner in every path of duty.

Meanwhile, our Saviour is represented as standing in the most intimate relation to his disciples yet on earth. His promise is: 'Where two or three are gatherered together in my name, there am I in the midst of them;* — Lo, I am

* Matt. xviii. 20.

with you always, even unto the end of the world.' * God 'gave him,' says St. Paul, 'to be the head over all things to the church.' † These and similar passages of Scripture seem to indicate that he is invisibly present with his church, and wields a delegated sovereignty over God's spiritual kingdom upon earth; in fine, that he stands in the same relation to the household of faith, in which the father of a family stands to his children, watching for their good, dispensing God's gifts to their necessities, their helper in every good work, the inspirer of holy thoughts, and of inward peace and joy.

Jesus is also spoken of as our intercessor with the Father. Says the writer to the Hebrews: 'He is able to save them to the uttermost that come unto God by him, seeing he ever liveth *to make intercession* for them. ‡ 'If any man sin,' says St. John, 'we have *an advocate* with the Father, Jesus Christ the righteous.'§ This intercession of Christ we regard with unfeigned and devout gratitude, not that we suppose it needed to render God propitious, but because it presents so vivid and touching an image of the Saviour's love for man.

Jesus is also spoken of as man's final judge; and the tribunal before which we must all appear, is designated as 'the judgment-seat of

* Matt. xxviii. 20 † Ephesians i. 22.
‡ Hebrews vii. 25. § 1 John ii. 1.

Christ.'* 'The Father hath committed all judgment unto the Son. . . . . The hour is coming, in the which all that are in the graves shall hear his voice, and shall come forth; they that have done good, unto the resurrection of life; and they that have done evil, unto the resurrection of damnation.'† This idea naturally connects itself with that of the intimate relation of Jesus to his church on earth, and to the assembly of the redeemed in heaven. The soul passes from the agony of death into his presence; and that very interview is in itself a judgment and a sentence. The soul, that is of his own lineage and kindred, sees its own cherished traits of character reflected from his countenance, and reads in his eye the invitation, 'Come, thou blessed of my Father.' On the other hand, the impenitent, the willingly guilty, from a countenance with which they have no sympathy, from a glance which reflects not theirs, receive the sad mandate, 'Depart ye cursed.' *Like or unlike him*, is the great question of the final judgment. This question, the ranks of spirits, as they go from earth to the Saviour's immediate presence, answer; and, as they answer it, join his heavenly flock, or go away into the company of outcasts and rebel spirits.

I would next refer to the idea entertained by many that our Saviour was God's agent in the

* 2 Corinthians v. 10. † John v. 22, 28, 29.

creation of the visible universe. Of this I find no scriptural proof. Indeed, the passages commonly quoted in support of this opinion, appear to me to have reference to something more precious and more enduring than the material universe, — to God's spiritual creation and kingdom. The idea under discussion rests mainly on two passages. One is in the Epistle to the Hebrews: 'By whom also he made the worlds.'* The word here rendered *worlds*, has for its primary meaning *ages* or *dispensations*. It is the word rendered *ages* in the following passage: 'The mystery which hath been hid from *ages* and from generations.' † I suppose that, in the passage under consideration, it means *ages*, namely, the successive ages of the church, or the different religious dispensations, patriarchal, Levitical and prophetical, which had preceded the advent of Christ. This exposition gives a peculiar force and beauty to the opening verses of the Epistle to the Hebrews: 'God, who at sundry times and in divers manners, spake unto the fathers by the prophets, hath in these latter days spoken unto us through his Son, whom he hath appointed heir of all things, on whose account he indeed made or arranged the earlier dispensations just referred to, making them all point onward to him, in all of them foreshadowing his coming and preparing the way.'

* Hebrews i. 2. † Colossians i. 26.

The other passage, in which it has been held Christ is distinctly set forth as the Creator of the universe, is this: 'For by, or through him were all things created, that are in heaven, and that are in earth, visible and invisible, whether they be thrones, or dominions, or principalities, or powers, all things were created by him, and for him; and he is before them all, and they are all bound together through him.' * This passage I understand as assigning to our Saviour much loftier functions, than the creation of a perishing universe. The *all things* referred to are the *thrones, principalities, and powers*, the ranks and distinctions in the spiritual universe, whether seen or unseen, whether apostles, pastors, and teachers, among dying men, or those, who occupy high places, nearest the throne, first in song, among the hosts of heaven. Their dignities, their thrones, and powers, are his creation, his gift. He ordains shepherds after his own heart on earth. He assigns to each his place, his sphere, in heaven. He is before them all, their prince, their head; and through him are they all bound together as one,—through him are they all, in heaven and on earth, made one family. With this exposition the verse next following fitly harmonizes. 'And he is the head of the body, the church.' This place, as prince and head of God's spiritual kingdom, the Scriptures with one voice

* Colossians i. 16, 17.

concede to him; and we gratefully reëcho the ascription of those in heaven, who cry, 'Worthy is the Lamb that was slain to receive power, and riches, and wisdom, and strength, and honor, and glory, and blessing.'

We arrive now at the important inquiry,— who, as to his person, was this wonderful being, in whom God thus enshrined and manifested himself, and who is now raised to the head of the spiritual universe? With regard to the person of Jesus, Unitarians are divided in sentiment. They are often accused of representing him as a *mere man;* but falsely. Those, who bear the name of Humanitarians, do not believe him to have been a man like other men; for, if he had no separate existence before his birth in Bethlehem, still the miraculous circumstances attending his birth, his intimate connection with the Deity, his vast endowments, his exalted mission, raised him far above all others, who have ever borne the human form. His apostles cannot at any time have regarded him as a *mere* man. They knew of his miraculous birth, of the vision of angels to the shepherds, of his preternatural wisdom in childhood, and of the voice from heaven at his baptism. They evidently never supposed him the supreme God. They always looked upon him as a fellow creature; but yet they manifestly regarded him as a superior being, and as one, of whom they could not have been surprised to learn, that he had existed before he came into this world.

Believing as I do, in our Saviour's preëxistence, I now ask your attention to some of the leading scriptural proofs, upon which this doctrine rests. I will first quote these words of our Saviour: 'No man hath ascended up to heaven, but *he that came down from heaven.*'* Is it said, that *coming down from heaven*, simply implies a divine commission? Why then did not John the Baptist, who certainly had a commission no less from God than that of Jesus, speak of himself as coming down from heaven? But he, in this same chapter, expressly speaks of Christ as coming from heaven, in a sense in which he himself did not come from heaven, and of himself as being of the earth, in a sense in which Christ was not of the earth. 'He must increase,' says the Baptist, 'but I must decrease. *He that cometh from above* is above all: he that is of the earth is earthly, and speaketh of the earth: *he that cometh from heaven* is above all.'

Again Jesus says of himself, 'What and if ye shall see the Son of man *ascend up where he was before?*'† When he uttered these words, he had just before called himself 'the bread which came down from heaven,' by which his Jewish hearers had understood him as asserting his preëxistence; for they immediately said

* John iii. 13. † John vi. 62.

among themselves: 'Is not this Jesus, the son of Joseph, whose father and mother we know? How is it then that he saith, I came down from heaven?' It is in the conversation induced by these cavils, that Jesus asks, 'What and if ye shall see the Son of man ascend up where he was before?'

I next cite the words of Jesus, '*Before Abraham was, I am.*'* Those, who deny our Saviour's preëxistence, regard these words as elliptical, and supply a second nominative after the verb *am*, 'Before Abraham was, I am' *he*,—I am the Christ, the Messiah, that is, I was marked out by a divine decree for the office of the Messiah, long before Abraham's birth. That in several instances in the New Testament, *he* must necessarily be supplied after *I am*, in order to complete the sentence, I freely admit. But in every one of these cases, (unless this constitute an exception,) *the Son of man*, or *the Christ*, or some synonymous word, or phrase, can be supplied from what immediately precedes. There is such an instance in this same chapter. 'When ye have lifted up the Son of man, then shall ye know that I am,' the *he* being necessarily supplied to complete the sentence, and referring to *the Son of man* (a title of the Messiah doubtless well known among the Jews,) immediately preceding. But in the text under discussion, if

* John viii. 58.

we supply the pronoun *he*, there is nothing which precedes, to which the pronoun can refer, no name or title of Jesus having been employed for more than *twenty* of the next preceding verses. I feel fully convinced, therefore, that there is no competent critical ground for translating this sentence, 'Before Abraham was, I am *he*.' But, even were we to deem this translation admissible on critical grounds, it makes our Saviour's words utterly unmeaning; and they might have been used by any other person, as well as by him. Peter, having existed from all eternity in the foreknowledge and determination of God, might have said, 'Before Abraham was, I am Peter,' with just as much truth and significance, as Jesus could have said, 'Before Abraham was, I am the Christ.' Moreover, these words of Jesus are in answer to the question: 'Thou art not yet fifty years old, and hast thou seen Abraham?' The answer ought, according to every reasonable principle of interpretation, to be understood as having some bearing upon the question.

I next quote the following, from our Saviour's prayer with his disciples: 'And now, O Father, glorify thou me with thine own self, *with the glory which I had with thee before the world was.*' And again, '*Thou lovedst me before the foundation of the world.*' * It requires bold and rash

* John xvii. 5, 24.

criticism to make this *glory before the world was*, a glory in the depths of divine counsels; and are we not borrowing from the scholastic absurdities of the middle ages, when we speak of God's love in anticipation for a non-existent being, — of his *love before the foundation of the world* for a being, who was not to see the light of life, till the world was four thousand years old? I know not how to evade the conclusion, that these passages denote our Saviour's preëxistence.

I will now adduce one or two passages from St. Paul. In his discourse on the resurrection, speaking of Christ, he says, 'The second man is *the Lord from heaven*.'* Here the whole argument is based on the heavenly origin and the superhuman character of Jesus.

St. Paul again says: 'Ye know the grace of our Lord Jesus Christ, that, *though he was rich*, yet for your sakes *he became poor*, that ye through his poverty might be rich.' The most obvious, and, to my mind, the only satisfying sense of these words is, that Jesus, for man's salvation, passed from a richer to a poorer, from a more lofty into a more humble condition.

These are some of the leading texts, which support the doctrine of our Saviour's preëxistence. There is something also in the general turn of the New Testament phraseology, with reference to him, for which I cannot account on

* 1 Corinthians xv. 47.

any other ground. I refer to the numerous passages, in which his advent is spoken of. Most of them, literally interpreted, would imply either his own antecedent personal agency, in connection with his advent, or, at least, his changing one state of being for another, rather than his beginning to exist. Such a passage is the following: 'He made himself of no reputation, (literally *emptied himself*, as if of what he had previously possessed or enjoyed,) and took upon him the likeness of men; and being found in fashion as a man, he humbled himself.' * To this class of texts, belongs also the following, from the Epistle to the Galatians: 'When the fulness of the time was come, God sent forth his Son, made of a woman. †

Some of the titles most usually given to our Saviour, seem to designate a personal rank superior to that of man, and according well with the idea of his preëxistence. The title, *Son of God*, implies, indeed, a created and subordinate being: and all men are, and are called, sons of God. But yet, it seems to be applied to our Saviour in a peculiar and exclusive sense, often with the distinguishing epithets *only* and *only-begotten.*

I might quote many other passages and considerations in confirmation of our Saviour's preexistence. I find many indubitable traces of it,

* Philippians ii. 7, 8. † Gal. iv. 4.

(particularly in the gospel of John,) which gain distinctness, the more closely I view them, and the more searchingly I apply to them the canons of sound criticism.

Were there but two or three passages, which seemed to teach this doctrine, and were it opposed to the general tenor of the New Testament, I should feel bound to interpret these few passages in accordance with the analogy of other Scriptures. But the passages are too various and too numerous to be regarded as merely figurative; and the doctrine, which they imply, in no wise militates against the language or the spirit of the New Testament in general. Indeed, there are considerations, which seem to render our Saviour's preëxistence intrinsically probable. The mission which he filled, was the loftiest that a created being could discharge; and it would seem reasonable, and natural, that, for so high a function, God should have ordained one of the elder, and more exalted members of his spiritual family, rather than one from the human race,— the youngest and humblest branch of that family.

Let me now notice briefly the principal objections urged against this doctrine.

In the *first* place, it is urged that Christ is not unfrequently styled *a man* in the New Testament. We answer, that he was 'found in fashion as a man,' passed through the vicissitudes of man's life, bore many of man's trials and infirmities, in fine, was, (whatever theory we adopt,) a man in very many of his circumstances and relations. Moreover, the analogy of Scripture gives us abundant reason to believe, that, with his preëxistence distinctly in view, the sacred writers would have frequently called him *a man*, when they contemplated him in his human aspects, relations, and fortunes. There are numerous instances, both in the Old and New Testament, in which superhuman beings are called *men*. Thus, in Genesis, we read of Abraham: 'The Lord appeared unto him in the plains of Mamre: and he sat in the tent-door in the heat of the day; and he lifted up his eyes and looked, and lo three *men* stood by him.'* In the next chapter, we are told of two of these *men:* 'There came two *angels* to Sodom,' and shortly after, of the same two, 'The *men* put forth their hand.' When the birth of Samson is announced, we first read that 'the *angel* of the Lord appeared unto the woman,'—then, that 'the woman came and told her husband, saying, A *man* of God came unto me,'—and lastly, that 'the *angel* of the Lord, (that is, the man of God just spoken of,) ascended in the flame of the altar.'† Luke, in describing our Lord's resurrection, says that 'two *men* stood by the women in shining gar-

* Genesis xviii. 1, 2. † Judges xiii. 3, 6, 20.

ments,'* which men John calls 'two *angels* in white.' These examples will suffice to show, that, in reasoning upon the nature of Christ, no stress can be laid on the mere use of the word *man*.

It is also objected to the doctrine of our Saviour's preëxistence, that it deprives his example of its appropriateness and value. By no means, I reply. All God's spiritual children are of the same family. Man is distinguished from other branches of the same family, less by nature, than by circumstances merely local and temporary. The duties incumbent on all created spirits, are the same, namely, love and obedience to the great Father spirit, love and charity to all fellow-spirits. The particular mode, in which these duties are to be discharged, depends upon the circumstances in which each individual spirit is placed; and, were the greatest of created spirits to be clothed with a human body, and to pass through an earthly life, his duties would be strictly human duties,—his conduct in any given situation, would be precisely what that of a common man, in the same situation, ought to be. Whatever, then, we may believe with regard to the nature of Christ, if he was 'found in fashion as a man,' his conduct, in all human relations, must have been precisely what man's ought to

* Luke xxiv. 4.

be, and must, therefore, be a fit example for our literal imitation. Nor let it be said, that, as superhuman, he was necessarily sinless; that he could not have felt the power of temptation; and that his victory over sin, therefore, affords us no encouragement. If he was a finite spirit, and a free agent, he must have been a subject of temptation, and capable of sin; and, though the miserable baits of earthly pleasure and ambition might have offered but little allurement to a heaven-born spirit, yet, in his superhuman endowments, and in his vastly expanded relations, and sphere of action, he might have found as strong temptations, as we do in the mere objects of sense, and might have won as arduous moral victories, as we should win, were we to lead an entirely stainless life from the cradle to the grave.

There is one thought, which, to my own mind, attaches a peculiar worth to our Saviour's example, on the ground of his preëxistence. I have said that all spirits are of one family. Outward circumstances alone, form the dividing line between good men and angels. 'In the resurrection, they are as the angels of God in heaven.' We are made for endless growth. In this life, 'it does not yet appear what we shall be;' but, unknown ages hence, we may look down upon the present spiritual attainments of an archangel, as we should look up to them now. We here are training ourselves in the school of Christ for familiar communion with the thrones, principalities, and powers of heaven. Does it not then commend itself to us as worthy of the infinite wisdom of our Father, that he should fit us for this blessed society, through the agency of one of these elder and purer spirits, whose exalted perfections may inspire us with an enthusiastic zeal as we seek to be his followers, while, looking to him as a brother, as one bound by the same ties, called to the same duties with ourselves, we may imitate him without despondency or discouragement?

Such are the views of our Saviour's person and character, which seem to me most consonant with the word of God. They commend themselves to my mind as equally removed from objectionable extremes. On the one hand, they bring the Saviour within the range of our sympathy, and save us from the inextricable confusion of ideas inseparable from the doctrine of the Trinity; and, on the other hand, they preserve unimpaired the matchless wisdom, the spotless purity, the divine authority of Jesus, and present him as a being, on whom we can look with mingled reverence and love, — whom we can welcome to our hearts as a brother, while we must bow before him as from a higher sphere, — who, at once, guides us in the duties of our mortal pilgrimage, and makes us, as partakers of his glory, peers of angels, and citizens of heaven.

While my reason and my heart are satisfied with these views, they constitute the only ground, on which I can make the voice of Scripture harmonize. The Trinitarian theory does great violence to the laws of interpretation, and brings the various testimonies of the divine word into harsh and irreconcilable conflict with each other. The Humanitarian expositions of Scripture, I dare not trust. They are lax. They seem to me to wrest the Scriptures. Though they have the advantage of being urged in behalf of a doctrine, not absurd, but in itself altogether tenable, in a critical point of view they seem to me hardly less objectionable, than the Trinitarian expositions do. The views, which I have now presented, do no violence, as I think, to the principles of sound criticism. I can go with them through the whole of the New Testament, and find not a text which gives me any serious difficulty. They suffer me to interpret the Scriptures in their literal and obvious sense, which neither of the other theories will. On this account, as one, who feels inadequate to settle these points without the authority of express revelation, and who receives the Scriptures as given by inspiration of God, I prize and cherish these views; and should be glad to know, that my statements and arguments have produced in your minds the same conviction that exists in my own.

I close with a single reflection. If this exalted being entered our world, assumed its burdens and its sorrows, and passed through its gates of death, of what momentous interest and importance must be the service which he came to render, — of what unspeakable worth, the salvation which he brings and offers! If, under a darker and less perfect dispensation, 'every transgression and disobedience received a just recompense of reward, how shall we escape, if we neglect so great salvation?'

LECTURE IV.

THE HOLY SPIRIT.

LUKE XI. 13.

IF YE THEN, BEING EVIL, KNOW HOW TO GIVE GOOD GIFTS UNTO YOUR CHILDREN, HOW MUCH MORE SHALL YOUR HEAVENLY FATHER GIVE THE HOLY SPIRIT TO THEM THAT ASK HIM?

THE HOLY SPIRIT is my subject this evening. I will commence my lecture by a word of explanation, which will be necessary for but few, yet which some may need. We sometimes read in the New Testament of the Holy *Spirit*, and full as often of the Holy *Ghost*. The original word is the same in one case, as in the other; but, at the time when the Bible was translated, *ghost* and *spirit* meant the same thing, and were used indifferently to express the same idea. Since that time the word *ghost* has become so restricted in its signification, as to denote only a *spectral apparition;* while *spirit* means the same now that it did then.

The controversy with regard to the Holy Spirit is, not as to its reality, or its divinity, but as to its *personality.* No Christian denies that there is a Holy Spirit, or maintains the Holy Spirit to be an inferior and subordinate person. But the Trinitarian maintains, that the Holy Spirit is a distinct and equal person of the Godhead. We, on the other hand, believe that the Holy Spirit is but a name, and a most appropriate name, for divine influences and operations, and, especially, for the influence of God upon the soul of man. In the present lecture, I shall first give you my reasons for not embracing the Trinitarian view of the Holy Spirit, and then shall expound and illustrate my own view of the nature and influences of the Holy Spirit.

I could name with great sincerity, as my first and sufficient reason for not embracing the Trinitarian doctrine on this subject, that I see not the shadow of an argument in support of it. I confess, that, while I cherish no disrespect for minds so constituted as to perceive the force of the arguments employed in defence of this doctrine, I myself am unable to appreciate them, and should hardly know how to refute them better than by a simple statement of them.

But, in pursuance of the plan marked out for these lectures, I shall go over the whole ground of the argument on both sides, as thoroughly as I can in a single discourse.

At the outset, in the way of regarding the Holy Spirit as a separate and independent person of the Godhead, there stand several scores of passages in the New Testament, in which the Holy Spirit is spoken of as subject to, or conferred by God and Christ. Such passages are the following: 'I will *put* my spirit upon him.'* 'How much more shall your heavenly Father *give* the Holy Spirit?'† 'God *giveth* not the spirit by measure unto him.'‡ 'God, who hath also *given* unto us his Holy Spirit.'§ 'The Holy Ghost *sent* down from heaven.'|| 'The Comforter, whom I will *send* unto you from the Father, even the spirit of truth.'¶ Who can send or give the supreme and eternal God? The very idea is unspeakably absurd.

I am aware of the usual mode of accounting for phraseology of the kind just quoted. It is maintained that the three equal persons of the Trinity entered into a covenant, by which the Son agreed to be subject to the Father, and the Holy Spirit to move at the bidding of the Father and the Son. But this covenant is not mentioned in the Bible. Moreover, it is a covenant of falsehood, — a covenant, by which the Son and the Holy Spirit agree to act a lie, — to represent a state of things which has no actual existence, — to play an assumed part. But, were we to admit this incongruous idea, (which I know not how to entertain for a moment,) of a cove-

* Matthew xii. 18. † Luke xi. 13. ‡ John iii. 34.
§ 1 Thess. iv. 8. || 1 Peter i. 12. ¶ John xv. 26.

nant between the three persons of the Godhead, I still should maintain, that, whatever reason existed for the assumed inferiority of the second and third persons, the same reason must needs exist for our receiving and regarding them in the characters which they have assumed. It is far more reverent and pious, to receive them as they are offered to us in the gospel, than to insist on rending off the disguise which they have chosen to wear, rescinding the covenant which they have sealed, and regarding them in a light in which they have agreed not to be regarded.

Again, were the Holy Spirit a person, especially a person of the Godhead, we should at least expect to find him designated by the use of a masculine noun, and masculine pronouns. We should hardly expect to find a divine person generally designated by a noun in the neuter gender, with articles, pronouns, adjectives, and participles in the neuter, (for, in the Greek, all these parts of speech are distinguished by gender.) Yet the Greek word rendered *spirit* or *ghost* is neuter, and is invariably connected with neuter articles, pronouns, adjectives, and participles. There is not an instance in which, in the Greek of the New Testament, a pronoun corresponding to our word *he*, *his*, or *him*, is used in connection with the Holy Spirit; but always a pronoun corresponding to *it* or *its*. Now, in the Greek language, the only cases, in which living beings are denoted by neuter nouns and pronouns, are those of certain diminutives, the smallness of which is expressed by the use of this gender,— an idiom like that, by which we, though in bad taste, call a very little child *it* instead of *he* or *she*. Is there then the slightest probability that the sacred writers should have employed the neuter gender to denote a person of the most exalted dignity,—a person of the Godhead?

But the Holy Spirit is, *four* times in the gospel of John, called the *comforter* or *advocate*, and in connection with this term, are employed words in the masculine gender; and, it is asked, must not that, which is called by a word so manifestly the name of a person, be a real person, and not a mere influence? I reply, that either the word *spirit*, and the neuter words used with it, are employed figuratively, or the word *comforter* is so employed. Now which is the most probable,—that this divine person should be spoken of literally in the New Testament but four times, and figuratively several hundreds of times, and that too in a figure, which diminishes, instead of amplifying his dignity; or, that a divine influence, which is spoken of literally several hundreds of times, should four times be personified? We must, in answering this question, bear it in mind, that the personifying of things without life, whether outward objects, or conceptions of the intellect, is an exceedingly common figure of speech, and one which always gives dignity to the things personified; while the opposite figure, namely, the use with regard to a person of language applicable to an inanimate object, is exceedingly rare, and is seldom employed, except in derision or irony, or to indicate the exceeding littleness of the person spoken of.

To show the true value of the argument for the personality of the Holy Spirit, based on the use of the word *comforter*, let us suppose a parallel case. Suppose that a volume of American sermons were put into the hands of a heathen, who understood our language, yet did not know the import of the word *Bible*. He would, it is to be hoped, often meet with that word, perhaps several times in each sermon. He would find it always treated as a neuter noun, and would see its place supplied by *it* and *which*, not by *he* and *who*. For the most part, there would be nothing said about the Bible, which was not literally applicable to a book. But in an exhortation towards the close of one of the sermons, something would perhaps be said about the duty of taking the Bible for a *guide;* and we will suppose the word *guide* used with regard to the Bible *four* times in this one passage. Now, were the heathen reader to insist that the Bible was a person, because in this volume of sermons it was *four* times called a *guide*, he would reason precisely like those, who infer the personality of the

Holy Spirit from the use of the word *comforter* concerning it, *four* times in a single discourse of our Saviour.

Again, any possible inference, which might be drawn in behalf of this doctrine of the personality of the Holy Spirit, from the use of the word *comforter*, is entirely precluded by the fact, that in each of the *four* instances,* in which this word is used, it is defined by the neuter noun *spirit*, with a variety of words in the neuter gender connected with it. The first instance reads thus: 'I will pray the Father, and he shall give you another Comforter, that he may abide with you forever, — even *the Spirit* of truth, *which* the world cannot receive, because it seeth *it* not, neither knoweth *it;* but ye know *it;* for *it* dwelleth with you, and shall be in you.' Every one of these pronouns in the original is in the neuter gender. The next instance reads thus: 'The Comforter, that is, *the Holy Spirit*, *which* the Father will send in my name,' the relative in the Greek being neuter. The next is this: 'When the Comforter is come, whom I will send unto you from the Father, even *the Spirit* of truth, *which* proceedeth from the Father.' In the fourth instance also, the Comforter is defined to be *the Spirit* of truth.

I would next remind you of other forms of speech in the New Testament, entirely incompatible with the personality of the Holy Spirit. The Holy Spirit is repeatedly said to be *poured*

*John xiv. 16, 26; xv. 26; xvi. 7.

out, *shed*, *quenched*, and the like, and Christians are said to be *anointed* with the Holy Spirit, — expressions never used with regard to persons, but entirely applicable when used with regard to influences.

Another most decisive argument against the distinct and personal divinity of the Holy Spirit, is to be found in the offices ascribed in the Scriptures to the Father, Son, and Holy Spirit, respectively. The Trinitarian theory is, that there is a partition of divine attributes and offices between the three persons, whose respective functions are intirely distinct and separate from each other. The Father is the Creator, the Son the Redeemer, the Holy Spirit, the Sanctifier. Now it might with much reason be objected to this partition, that the two last-named offices are one; that sanctification is man's only redemption; that sin is precisely what Jesus came to save men from; and that he can do this only by making them holy. But we will not insist on this. We will suppose these three offices of Creator, Redeemer, and Sanctifier, in themselves entirely distinct from each other. Now if it appears that the three persons of the Godhead (so called) discharge each other's alleged functions, the distinction of persons can be no longer maintained. This, I think, will appear: and, in particular, we shall see that sanctification, deemed the special function of the Holy Spirit, is ascribed both to the Father and to the Son;

and on the other hand, that creation and redemption, regarded as the prerogatives of the Father and the Son, are ascribed to the Holy Spirit.

Sanctification is ascribed to the Father. In a prayer addressed expressly to the Father, Jesus says: 'Sanctify them through thy truth.'* St. Paul prays: 'The very God of peace sanctify you wholly.'† St. Jude addresses his epistle 'to them that are sanctified by God the Father.'‡

Sanctification is also attributed to Jesus. Says St. Paul: 'Of him are ye in Christ Jesus, who of God is made unto us wisdom, and righteousness, and sanctification.'§ And, again: 'Christ also loved the church and gave himself for it, that he might sanctify and cleanse it.'‖ Says the writer to the Hebrews: 'We are sanctified through the offering of the body of Christ once for all.'¶ And, again: 'Jesus also, that he might sanctify the people with his own blood, suffered without the gate.'**

To the Holy Spirit also, creation, the Father's alleged prerogative, is ascribed, as in these passages: 'By his Spirit he hath garnished the heavens.'†† 'The Spirit of God hath made me, and the breath of the Almighty hath given me life.'‡‡

Every stage also in Christ's work of redemp-

* John xvii. 16. † 1 Thess. v. 23. ‡ Jude i. 1.
§ 1 Cor. i. 30. ‖ Ephesians v. 25, 26. ¶ Heb. x. 10. 11.
** Heb. xiii. 12. †† Job xxvi. 13. ‡‡ Job xxxiii. 4.

tion is ascribed to the Holy Spirit. He ascribes his own miracles to 'the Spirit of God;'* and he is said to have offered himself through the eternal Spirit.' †

The Scriptures then leave no ground for the distinction of attributes and offices between the three persons of the Trinity, claimed by our Trinitarian friends; and, in ascribing to the Holy Spirit the same, and only the same attributes and offices ascribed to the Father and the Son, they make the distinct personality of the Holy Spirit a theory utterly without foundation.

The texts, usually quoted in support of the personality of the Holy Spirit, are those in which the Holy Spirit is spoken of as being *sent*, *blasphemed*, *tempted*, *grieved* or *resisted*, all which are not unusual instances of personification, and represent a style of language constantly employed with regard to objects without life. Thus we say that a *shower is sent*, that *divine mercy is blasphemed*, that one's *integrity is tempted*, that *good counsels are resisted.*

The only text that demands distinct notice is the following: 'Likewise the Spirit also helpeth our infirmities; for we know not what we should pray for as we ought: but the Spirit itself maketh intercession for us with groanings which cannot be uttered. And he that searcheth the hearts knoweth the mind of the Spirit, because it

* Matt. xii. 28. † Heb. ix. 14.

maketh intercession for the saints according to the will of God.'* It is surprising that this text should ever have been quoted as favoring the idea of the supreme, independent divinity of a spirit, which *intercedes*, that is, offers prayer, of course to some superior being; nor does the idea of *groaning* accord with the serene and perfect happiness of an almighty being. I do not think, that the Spirit of God is referred to in this passage. It is the spirit or soul of *man*, of the *Christian*, that is here spoken of. The apostle has alluded, in the preceding verses, to the infirmities of an earthly condition, which are to be borne with patience and hope. He adds: 'The Spirit, the soul, also, fixed on God and on eternal things, helps our infirmities, — sustains our frail bodies. We indeed often know not what is best for us, — what we ought to pray for; but the soul still prays, — pours itself out to God in aspirations and longings, deep and fervent, though often vague and indefinite. And he that searches the hearts of men, knows the mind of the Spirit, — knows the meaning of its groans and supplications, — knows the wants, which it does not know itself; for the souls of the righteous intercede for them according to the divine will, — long and yearn, in these groanings that cannot be uttered, for such spiritual favors, as God is always ready to bestow.' The idea of

* Rom. viii. 26, 27.

the passage is, that the devout soul, in all its infirmity and its ignorance, will still be sustained, for it will still press to the mercy-seat; and that if it knows not even what to ask for, and cannot shape its own supplications, God, knowing the rectitude and earnestness of its desires, will satisfy all its real wants.

The Holy Spirit is not then a distinct person. What is it? What does the phrase mean? How are we to account for its use? We shall not, it seems to me, need to look far for our answer. Our common use of the word *spirit* will sufficiently explain its use in the sacred writings. What do we mean by the *spirit* of a man? A man performs two kinds of works,— exerts two kinds of agency. Some things he does expressly,—visibly, or audibly,—by word, or hand, or writing. Other, and often much greater things, he brings to pass by his influence, —by silent outgoings from his character,—by the power of his example,—by an agency, which far transcends his sphere of immediate action, and often outlasts the period of his mortal life. This influence, this agency, we usually denominate the *spirit* of the man; and its effects, its fruits, whether in the character of individuals or in the state of society, we also designate as his *spirit*. For instance, we call the influence, which the efforts and example of Howard the philanthropist had, and still have, the *spirit* of Howard;

and, whenever we see works like his wrought, or persons engaged in works like his, we say that the *spirit* of Howard is in those works, or in those men. We then habitually use the word *spirit* to designate, *first*, a man's *influence*, and *secondly*, *the effects of that influence.*

Now I conceive that we have no need of going beyond these common, well known uses of the word *spirit*, to explain its use in the Scriptures with reference to the Almighty. We find the phrases, *Spirit of God*, *Spirit of truth*, *Holy Spirit*, and the like, constantly used in these senses; and there is not a passage, as seems to me, in which it is necessary to look farther for a signification both obvious and satisfying.

The *Spirit of God*, the *Holy Spirit*, and like phrases, most frequently denote simply the divine influence, sometimes in creation, and in outward events, but, in the great majority of instances, on the soul of man. They denote indeed a great diversity of divine influences, just as, by the spirit of a man, we denote every variety of influence which a human being can exercise. We trace the spirit of a man in the building of a city, in the planning of a voyage, in the diffusion of literary taste, in the establishment of any public institution, in the tone of moral feeling cherished by his influence, in ideas or sentiments, to which he gave the first development; in fine, in any way, in which, without his direct bodily action, his character has impressed itself on objects, events, or the minds and hearts of others. An equally wide ground does the phrase *Spirit of God*, with its cognate phrases, cover. It is used with reference to the plenary inspiration and the power from on high, which rested upon Jesus. To him, we are told, God 'gives not his Spirit by measure;' but on him bestows every form of divine influeuce and endowment, of which a created being is capable. Then it is used concerning the peculiar communications of light and power vouchsafed to the apostles and their converts. Those, who were thus endowed, were always said to have received the Holy Spirit. It is used of particular divine intimations and impressions, as when the Spirit bade Philip join the Ethiopian, and sent Peter to the house of Cornelius. Then, too, it is often used, as is our text, to denote those aids in the religious life, which 'whosever asks, receives, and he that seeks, finds.' And it is used, in all these cases, with regard both to the influence and its effects; that is, it is employed to designate the spiritual gifts of God, both as they come from him, and as they rest upon the minds and hearts of men.

Now it is self-evident that there is the same room for the use of this phraseology with reference to God, that there is with reference to man. There is the same distinction between the modes and forms of divine action, that there is with reference to the deeds and agency of man. There are some things, which God confers, utters, or brings to pass, visibly or audibly. There are other things, which he gives or brings to pass silently, without any interposing cause that can be seen or traced; and all the various influences of this kind, with their results or effects, are what are termed in the Scriptures the *Holy Spirit.*

But, while we find no ground in reason or Scripture for believing in the personality of the Holy Spirit, we regard the influence of God upon the soul of man as an indisputable, essential, fundamental doctrine of religion. What distinguishes us from our Trinitarian brethren on this point, is, that we regard this influence as flowing, not from a fragment of the divine nature, but from the whole undivided Deity. And least of all, can we sympathize with believers in the Trinity, in separating God the Father from the divine influence upon the soul. We feel that it is peculiarly in his fatherly relation and attributes, that God is present with the soul of man. We find the full promise of the Holy Spirit in these words of Jesus: 'If a man love me, he will keep my words; and my Father will love him, and we will come unto him, and make our abode with him.' It is the Spirit of the Father, and the Son, and this alone, that we desire and seek, not a Spirit in any respect or degree distinct from either the Father or the Son.

Let me employ the few moments, for which I yet can claim your attention, in developing what I conceive to be the scriptural doctrine of spiritual influences.

In the first place, the Spirit of God is in his works. We accord in full with the declaration of the Wisdom of Solomon: 'Thine incorruptible Spirit is in all things.' Well has it been said: 'This fair universe, were it in the meanest province thereof, is in very deed the star-domed city of God. Through every star, through every grass-blade, the glory of a present God still beams. Nature is the time-vesture of God.' With equal truth and beauty, does Goethe put into the mouth of the earth-spirit the words: —

> 'Tis thus at the roaring loom of life I ply,
> And weave for God the garment thou see'st Him by.'

Our first parents heard the voice of the Lord God in the garden; and they, no doubt miraculously, but not one whit more distinctly than we may hear it this very night. There is no poetical fancy, but literal truth in the beautiful words of the hymn just sung: —

> 'Hark! on the evening breeze,
> As once of old, the Lord God's voice
> Is heard among the trees.'

Such is the constant testimony of Scripture. God is spoken of as actively present in all the forms and agencies of the outward universe.

Does a tempest rise? 'He maketh the winds his angels.' Do the thunders roll? 'The voice of the Lord is upon the waters; the God of glory thundereth.' Do showers bless the harvest field? 'He watereth the hills from his chambers.' Does verdure clothe the plain? 'He causeth the grass to grow for the cattle, and herb for the service of man.' And in all these forms, in myriads of ways, is he speaking to the hearts of his human family, claiming their worship, casting deep reproach upon their coldness and indifference, and awakening in every thoughtful soul the resolution of the Psalmist: 'I will sing unto the Lord as long as I live: I will sing praise unto my God while I have my being. My meditation of him shall be sweet: I will be glad in the Lord.' There is, I believe, a perpetual communion on God's part with man, in the order, harmony, beauty and majesty of creation. I believe, that I no more truly address loving words day by day to the children dearer to me than my own soul, than God has this day directly spoken to each and all of us, his children, in the sunshine and the flowers, in the mellow twilight and the gentle breeze. I sincerely believe, that the express design of this fair and wonderful creation is to bring the Creator near, and to make his presence felt by the living souls of men, — to supply a medium of communication between the Infinite and the finite, — to render visible and audible those thoughts of love, fathomless as the ocean, numberless as its sands.

In the same light do I regard the whole course of Providence. The events of life, ordered by the close and constant care of the Almighty, have each a voice from him for the spirit's ear, a lesson of truth, a message of duty, a word of warning or rebuke, comfort or encouragement. How near, how incessant the watchful presence indicated by our Saviour's words: 'The hairs of your head are all numbered.' In the mercies so thickly strewn along our daily path, are fulfilled, in every one of our thoughtless moments, the words of Holy Writ: 'God hath spoken once, yea, twice, but man perceiveth it not.' In every sorrow comes the voice: 'Hear ye the rod, and who hath appointed it.'

But, yet more, apart from outward forms and events, I believe in the intimate presence and communion of God with the soul of man. His hand-writing is on our innermost shrines of thought; his voice thrills through the deepest recesses of our being. As the builder of a house may construct for himself a secret passage, opening by springs which no one else can find, so has the Almighty architect of the soul of man reserved his own hidden avenues of access, by which he visits the soul in its days of gladness and its night seasons of sorrow, in its health and its sickness, giving it meat to eat, of which the world knows not, letting in the day-spring from on high upon its darkened chambers, filling with the oil of joy its empty and shrunken vessels. None can shut out the thoughts that God sends; but, unsought, unsuggested by the ordinary laws of association; nay, often unwelcome, they remain, return, haunt the soul, knock at the heart's door, and often forsake it not, till they are cherished and obeyed. How true to human experience are the Psalmist's words: 'Whither shall I go from thy Spirit?' Not we ourselves can hold so close communion with our own souls, as God can; for how often does his Spirit reverse our own inward thoughts, and say the opposite of what we were saying within ourselves! We are whispering peace to our souls; but the Spirit cries, in a voice which self-delusion cannot drown, 'No peace without repentance and the fruits of love.' We flatter ourselves that we are rich and full; but the Spirit cries, 'Nay, — ye are poor and naked, hungry and thirsty, — come, drink of my cup, and eat of my bread, and put on my beautiful garments.' Or, on the other hand, though in the way of duty, we doubt and fear; and, in the hour of sad self-communion, the Spirit enters, and says, 'Peace be with you,' and the cloud rises from our souls and melts away, our hearts grow warm, and burn within us, and we perceive that it is the Lord.

Whence too, when we have trodden the path of transgressors, those unsought warnings, presentiments of evil, forebodings of penalties that we have defied? Whence that uneasy, restless feeling, that will ever intrude itself, when we linger too long on the roadside of our heavenward pilgrimage, when we forsake duty for pleasure, when we serve Mammon instead of God? Whence those preparation seasons for the trial of faith or virtue which every Christian has experienced,—seasons, when, without any outward cause, impressions have been borne in upon our minds, spiritual exercises have been induced, and views and purposes cherished, precisely adapted to exigencies just at hand, yet unforeseen, as if our Father, when he saw the storm gathering, had hastened to wrap us beforehand in the mantle of his love, and to set our feet in a straight and safe path? Whence that serene satisfaction, that joy in the Lord, that inward repose and harmony, which flow from trials well sustained and duties nobly done, and which give us the surest foretaste of heaven that we can have below? Has there ever been a day, whether of duty or of sin, of joy or of sorrow, of levity or of seriousness, when, if we had strictly reviewed our heart's history for the day, we should not have been constrained to confess that God had been there, and that his Spirit had borne witness, either with, or against our spirits? No. The divine

Spirit has always sought to draw us. God has been unceasingly near. 'Behold I stand at the door and knock,' is his voice to each of us. There lives not the man, who has ever succeeded in shutting God from his heart. Though we take the wings of the morning, he is before us. Though the darkness cover us, it hides us not from him.

It is of these influences of the divine Spirit upon the soul of man, that it is written, 'Quench not the Spirit,'—'Grieve not the Holy Spirit of God.' For these influences, the Scriptures teach us, are not irresistible; but, like the counsels or the influence of a faithful human parent or friend, may be disobeyed and disregarded.

To these same scriptural influences, welcomed and obeyed, the Scriptures ascribe all that is good and holy in man,—all the graces and virtues of the regenerate heart. It is by the help of God, that we discharge our duty, that we grow in grace, that we become followers of Jesus,—all which is sufficiently indicated in such Scriptures as these: 'By the grace of God I am what I am.'—'It is God that worketh in you to will and to do of his good pleasure.'—'As many as are led by the Spirit of God, they are the sons of God.'—'The Spirit of God dwelleth in you.' In accordance with this idea of the helping Spirit of God, as essential to the Christian life, those, who yield themselves to the divine influence, are styled 'born of the Spirit,'—'baptized with the Holy Spirit;' and are said to 'walk after the Spirit,' to 'live in the Spirit,' and to 'have the Spirit of God resting upon them.'

Such is the Christian doctrine of the *Holy Spirit*,—the influence of God in nature, in providence, and, more than all, his direct, immediate influence upon the heart of man,—not a constraining, irresistible influence, but an influence, which may, on the one hand, be grieved and quenched; or, on the other, welcomed and obeyed; and which, if yielded to, becomes the source of everything worthy and holy in the character,—the fountain of renewed and sanctified affections, and of a Christ-like walk and conversation.

For this spirit, for these influences, prayer prepares the soul, so as to render them availing and enduring. By prayer man opens the door of his heart to the Spirit, that always seeks an entrance and a home there; nor can any earthly parent so promptly meet the wants of an only child, as God, by his ever present Spirit, fulfils the desires of the praying soul.

I am happy to believe, that, with regard to these fundamental, practical views of spiritual influences, there is no essential difference among Christians. On this subject, the religious phraseology of Christians of different modes of faith, for the most part, coincides; and all true religious experience must, of necessity, be coincident. This experience of the welcomed influences and the blessed fruits of the Spirit, may God grant us all, through Jesus Christ our Saviour.

LECTURE V.

HUMAN NATURE.

ECCLESIASTES VII. 29.

LO, THIS ONLY HAVE I FOUND, THAT GOD HATH MADE MAN UPRIGHT; BUT THEY HAVE SOUGHT OUT MANY INVENTIONS.

HUMAN NATURE, as it now is, will be our subject of inquiry this evening. And, as it is my chief purpose, in these lectures, to discuss topics, on which we differ more or less widely from our fellow Christians, I will define at the outset the view of human nature, commonly termed *total depravity.* The fairest mode of doing this is by quotations from the Assembly's Catechism, which is still accepted as the standard of doctrine in the Calvinistic Churches of Great Britain and America. The words of this catechism, which I will not undertake to interpret, are as follows : 'God created man in his own image, in knowledge, righteousness, and holiness, with dominion over his creatures. When God created man, he entered into a covenant with him upon condition of perfect obedience, forbidding him to eat of the tree of knowledge of good and evil, upon pain of death. Our first parents, being left to the freedom of their own will, fell from the estate wherein they were created, by sinning against God. The covenant being made with Adam, not only for himself, but for his posterity, all mankind, descending from him by ordinary generation, sinned in him, and fell with him in the first transgression. The sinfulness of that state, whereinto man fell, consists in the guilt of Adam's first sin, the want of original righteousness, the corruption of his whole nature, which is commonly called original sin, together with all the actual transgressions which proceed from it. All mankind by the Fall lost communion with God, are under his wrath and curse, and so made liable to all the miseries in this life, to death itself, and to the pains of hell forever. This constitutes the misery of that estate, whereinto man fell.' Though this jargon is still acknowledged as the standard of faith, probably very few in our own community would pretend to interpret it, or would own themselves believers in the appalling consequences, which might be derived from it. There are perhaps few, who would assert, in so many words, that the unconscious infant lies under God's wrath and curse, and is, by virtue of his birth into the world, without any sinful act of his own, liable to the pains of hell forever. But it is now generally maintained by those called Calvinists, *first*, that human nature sustained a radical change after Adam's first transgression; *secondly*, that Adam, as the representative, (*the federal head*, as their phrase is,) of the whole human family, involved all his posterity in his own guilt; and, *thirdly*, that in some sense or degree men are now born sinners. These propositions demand, each a separate examination.

1. It is maintained, that *human nature sustained a radical change after Adam's first transgression*. This, if true, is a historical fact, of which we might with reason expect to find some record in the Bible. We, however, look in vain for it. The Mosaic narrative says nothing of such a change. Man's place of residence was indeed changed. He was driven from Eden, and a life of labor was appointed him. But would he have been left in indolence, had he been innocent? Labor is the fundamental law of all spiritual worth and progress; and we cannot suppose, that if a man had not transgressed, he would have been exempt from it. God could never have designed an earthly paradise for man's permanent abode. The law, 'subdue the earth,' which was a law of arduous labor, was given before the fall; and the garden of Eden was but the cradle of man's intellectual infancy, in which he was fostered, till he became sufficiently conversant with outward objects, to

manage his own affairs with discretion. Had he not sinned, he would still, for his own sake, have been removed from the garden, though he would have sought the wilderness in a more cheerful and hopeful spirit, than that, in which, after his transgression, he entered upon the stern, yet salutary discipline of a laborious life. But when he went forth, no curse was uttered upon him, or upon the partner of his guilt. The condition of mortal life was unfolded to them; but it was not so much as hinted, that its condition would have been essentially otherwise, had they remained innocent. Indeed, the very appointments of toil and physical suffering are those, on which the blessing of God most manifestly rests, — those, from which proceeds the surest growth of virtue and piety, — those, on which the divine example of the innocent Saviour sheds its brightest rays. But, could it be maintained that man's *condition* on earth was essentially modified by Adam's sin, still this would prove nothing with regard to his *nature:* nor can it be pretended, that there is the slightest allusion in the Bible to the change of his nature, as a historical fact.

But the change of man's nature is inferred from the earliness and frequency of human guilt ever since Adam, — from the fact that sins are among the first acts of every man's moral agency. But the eating of the forbidden fruit is the only recorded act of Adam's and Eve's moral agency.

They yielded to the first temptation, when surrounded by what seemed to be constraining motives to obedience. Certainly there never was a first sin so wanton, or so difficult to be accounted for as theirs. Of every other tree in the garden they might eat. The express voice of God had charged them not to eat of this. Gratitude, hope, fear, all conspired to insure their obedience. But they fell as soon as they were tempted. What more have their children done? Their sin was of the same kind with most of the sins of their posterity, that is, the yielding of principle to impulse,—the seizing of a momentary gratification, without thought, at the time, of duty or of consequences. If the sins of their posterity, then, prove their nature to be depraved, equally does the first transgression of Adam and Eve prove, that they were created with a depraved nature. There is, in the case of our first parents, and in that of their posterity, an identity, which militates strongly against the idea of any change of nature after the fall.

2. It is maintained by our Calvinistic brethren, that *Adam, as the representative or federal head of his posterity, involved them all in the guilt of his first transgression.* This doctrine assumes for its basis the following alleged facts. *God made at the outset a covenant with Adam in behalf of all mankind, the conditions of which covenant were, that, if Adam remained innocent, he and all his*

posterity should enjoy eternal life, but that, if he sinned, he and all his posterity should go into everlasting punishment. Adam consented thus to stand for the whole race. They all, therefore, sinned in and through him as their head or representative. This is expressly the doctrine of the Assembly's Catechism. It is almost too absurd to demand an answer; and might, at first thought, seem too revolting to our instinctive notions of right and justice, to deserve a respectful treatment. But it has been, and still is believed by many worthy and good men; and therefore ought not to be passed over in silence, or with sneers.

It seems a fatal objection to the doctrine just stated, that no mention is made in the Bible of a covenant between God and Adam; nor is the slightest hint anywhere given of Adam's acting in behalf of his posterity. Then again, Adam ad no right to act in their behalf. A representative must be authorized, — *he* was not authorized. You and I never gave him a *power of attorney* to obey or sin in our stead; nor is it in the nature of things possible, that we should be morally responsible for his acts. We may indeed feel their consequences; but we cannot be involved in their guilt, unless we authorized him to act for us.

Yet again, supposing that Adam had had the power of making such a covenant, his making it would have been his first transgression, and a sin infinitely more heinous than his eating the forbidden fruit, nay, a sin, for which his name ought to be forever accursed among men. Suppose that I had the power of covenanting, that, whatever sins I might commit, they should impart a guilty taint to my remotest posterity, would you not think me less a man, than a fiend, to consent to such a covenant?

The only passage of Scripture commonly quoted in support of this idea of Adam's *federal headship*, is that, where St. Paul says, that, 'as by one man sin entered into the world, and death by sin, even so death passed upon all men, for that all have sinned;' and also, that 'by one man's disobedience many were made sinners.'* But the whole of the sentence last quoted, is, 'For as by one man's disobedience many were made sinners, so by the obedience of one shall many be made righteous.' Now, how are *many made righteous by Christ's obedience?* Manifestly, by copying it, and in no other possible way, — by feeling its influence, and obeying its example. In like manner, (if there is any force in the apostle's comparison,) are *many made sinners by Adam's disobedience*, by following it, by imitating it, by yielding to like temptations. But, in this same connection, the apostle says,

* Romans v. 12–19.

that 'death reigned from Adam to Moses, even over them that had not sinned after the similitude of Adam's transgression,' by whom, Doddridge, (whose orthodoxy as a critic none will question,) says, and rightly, as I think, that infants were intended. Now, if Adam sinned in behalf of his posterity, infants, having sinned in and through him, could not have been excluded by the apostle from a share in his guilt. Moreover, this phrase, *the similitude of Adam's transgression*, is of prime importance, as defining the sense of the whole passage. The human race in general is here spoken of by St. Paul, as somehow connected with the sin of their first parent. The apostle speaks of some, who are not thus connected, and describes them as not having 'sinned after the similitude of Adam's transgression.' The inference is irresistible, that the rest of mankind were spoken of as connected with Adam's sin, because they had 'sinned after the similitude of his transgression,' and that their connection with him was that of similarity or imitation. Let it be also borne in mind, that this 'similitude of Adam's transgression' could not have existed in any of his posterity, if the race had undergone a change of nature; but the *similitude* did, and does exist, if his posterity, with a nature as pure as his, have in general fallen into sin as wantonly and as promptly as he did.

Once more, the idea of Adam's having bound the whole race in the guilt of his first trangression is opposed to very many express declarations of holy writ, of which it may be sufficient to quote the following, than which I can conceive of nothing more decisive. 'The son shall not bear the iniquity of the father, neither shall the father bear the iniquity of the son: the righteousness of the righteous shall be upon him, and the wickedness of the wicked shall be upon him.' *

3. It is maintained, (and perhaps the idea in the minds of many professed believers in man's native depravity, may amount to little more than this,) that *men are in some sense or degree born sinners*, — that every man comes into the world *depraved*, that is, averse from all that is good, and inclined to all that is evil. With regard to this notion, the first question is, — is God the creator of every individual human being that is now born, so that men and women of the present day may, in any proper sense, be termed his workmanship and his offspring? If so, and if man be born depraved, then does God create that, which is positively bad and evil, — that, which is utterly opposed to his will and law, — that, in which he can take no pleasure, — that, which he must needs view from the first with

* Ezekiel xviii. 20.

positive displeasure and abhorrence. Now it is the height of absurdity to maintain, that an Almighty being can create what he hates and abhors, or that an infinitely good and holy being can create what is essentially evil and vile. It is intrinsically necessary, that whatever God creates should be good, very good, perfect in its kind and for its purpose. What he creates must necessarily be the transcript of his own ideas, and therefore pure as he is pure; nor can I conceive of a fouler blasphemy, than to ascribe to the eternal Father the authorship of what is intrinsically vile and hateful.

But I apprehend that the advocates of the popular doctrine of depravity are not, in general, chargeable with this blasphemy. Their phraseology would seem to imply, that God was the Creator of Adam and Eve only, — that he is not in any proper sense the Creator of the men and women that now are, — that the Greek poet was mistaken, when he said, 'For we are also His offspring.' They attribute to Adam, rather than to God, the authorship of human nature as it now is. But I am content to rest the truth, that *God is the Creator and Father of all men*, on the simple doctrine of a paternal Providence as revealed in the Bible. I cannot believe, that they, the hairs of whose heads are all numbered, that they, who are bidden to dismiss all doubt and care because God careth for them, are thus dependent on any other being than their Maker, — are thus kept and blest by any other than their Father. And, if God be their Maker and their Father, I know that their nature must be good, however frail, and however much they may have perverted it.

I have thus attempted to analyze, and to refute in detail, the popular doctrine of depravity. There are, however, several general observations to be made upon it.

The idea of native depravity is opposed to our own consciousness. We do not feel as if sin were natural to us. There are portions of our nature, that always rise up against it. We always feel, that we were made for something better. We are stung with self-reproach when we sin, which could not be the case, were sin natural; for whatever is in accordance with nature must needs be satisfying and agreeable to the nature, with which it accords. We never sin without a motive, whereas, were we natively depraved, we should sin spontaneously and from the mere love of sin. Bad men, the worst men, never sin for the sake of sinning; but act kindly and do right, when they are not expressly urged to sin by appetite or passion. You may ask your way to a particular place, of the vilest sinner living ; and, unless he has some immediate motive for misleading you, he will point out the right way with a minuteness and assiduity proportioned to the intricacy of the road, and to the inconvenience which might result from your not finding it. Do you not suppose, that it is one of the rarest of events for a man to be in any such matter misdirected or deceived, from the mere caprice of wickedness, without some special motive of cupidity or revenge? Yet, were men natively depraved, they would be perpetually misguiding and circumventing each other, for the mere love of evil; and it would require a selfish motive, in order for an unregenerate man to tell the truth, or to perform the most common act of neighborly courtesy or kindness.

Those who have been most familiar with crime, your Howards, your Fryes, and your Tuckermans, those who dive down into the lowest depth of depravity to seek and save its victims, will tell you, that they find none utterly depraved; and that, even among those, who have been strangers to every humanizing influence, who have been born and brought up in the most pestilential atmosphere, and within the very gates of death, there are to be traced the filaments of noble powers and lofty sentiments. They will bring forth for you, from among the offscourings of all things, as we are too prone to deem them, striking traits and instances of sympathy, pity, persevering kindness, fidelity, self-sacrifice. They will tell you of a quick moral sensibility and a tender conscience among these outcasts, with regard to the few things, in which their duty has been made known to them. They will tell you of yearnings and aspirations for goodness and for purity, even in the dens of the grossest pollution. And do not all these things betoken a nature made in the image of God, and noble still in its debasement and defilement? Such developments of character cannot be traced to any kind or degree of moral culture; for they are often witnessed where there has been no culture, but, on the other hand, every possible form and mode of vicious example and influence from the cradle. The elements of good, that are found in persons thus trained, God must have lodged in their natures, as they came from his hands, — else they are an effect without any assignable cause.

The phenomena of infancy and childhood also, rebut the idea of native depravity. There is, in the young spirit, a simplicity, and ingenuousness, which can bear no kindred with a sinful nature. In the fountain of being, as it first rises, there is a transparent purity, which indicates that it can gush from no polluted source. The moral sensibilities of young children are always in the right direction; their moral intuitions marvellously clear and true. They are, indeed, easily and often led astray, — their impulses are strong, their power of resistance weak; yet the prompt tear of penitence when they sin, and the panting earnestness, with which they hasten to seek forgiveness of their human parents, and, when rightly directed, of their Father in heaven, sufficiently show 'the work of the law written in their hearts.' And how quick do their eyes glisten at the recital of a good deed,—how strong their loathing for all that is ungenerous, base, and vile! How free their love,—how slow their hatred, even under unkind or harsh treatment! The closer my acquaintance with little children, with the more utter horror and loathing do I turn from the remotest approach to the doctrine of native depravity. I feel, when with little children, that I am very near the pure fountain of life. They seem to me fresh from the baptism of a Father's blessing. I see his signature on their innocent brows, on their guileless spirits. I can sympathize in full with the beautiful words of a favorite poet:—

'A boundless wealth of love and power
  In the young spirit lies,—
Love, to enfold all natures
  In one benign embrace,—
Power, to diffuse a blessing wide
  O'er all the human race!'

But to think that there is depravity in those young spirits, as God sends them forth,—to think that there is more of evil than of good in what we, parents, are accustomed to hail as God's best gift,—to believe that there is a frown of divine displeasure, a sentence of damnation, hanging over the sweet babe,—to believe that the child, as yet incapable of discerning between good and evil, can even need pardon or redemption,—oh, it would separate me from my little ones. I would sooner go into the wilderness, and live a hermit, than look upon them with the eye, with which I must view them, did I believe that either God or Adam had made them sinners. Not mine should be the hopeless, despairing task, of attempting to repair the work, which God had sent into the world defiled and ruined.

The idea of man's being born a sinner will also appear unreasonable, when we consider the nature of sin. 'Sin is the transgression of the law.' The very idea of sin implies wrong volition on the part of the sinner. A thing or being may be, by nature, defective, ill-constructed; but sin must be a matter of personal choice.

But, could we admit as possible the doctrine of native depravity, it would render sin in its active forms impossible, or rather, it would make that, which we now call goodness, sin. The utmost that can be expected or demanded of any person, is, that he should be and do what, in his very nature, God has fitted him to be and do. The nature of a person includes all his perceptions, instincts, impulses, powers, and faculties. In a sinful nature, these must all be evil, so that to do evil would be the right and appropriate work of such a nature; while, in order to be or to do good, it must violate the fitness of things, depart from the analogy of other beings, and thwart the purposes of its creation. A sinful nature and accountability for moral evil cannot coexist. If God has given me a sinful nature, he gave it to me with the design and expectation that I should do evil, and evil only. I may then say with perfect fitness,

'Evil, be thou my good;'

and, if I can claim any praise or benefit at God's hands, it will be for cultivating and exercising my evil propensities, for making myself as bad as I can, and doing as much evil as I can. If he has given me an evil nature, I should offend him and incur his just displeasure, by trying to be good or to do good. If I am blameworthy, and penally accountable to God, for my sins, (and my own conscience and the word of God both tell me that I am,) it must be because he has given me a nature fitted for duty and for goodness.

The Scriptural argument for man's native depravity is almost too slender to claim attention. The leading proof-text for this doctrine has already been made the subject of discussion. I know of but two others, which it is necessary to notice. One is the expression of David: 'I was shapen in iniquity; and in sin did my mother conceive me.'* One must strangely misapprehend the design and spirit of this Psalm, in looking to it for an explicit, formal statement of theological dogmas. This Psalm was the expression of David's intense anguish and remorse for one of the most flagitious crimes, with which a human being was ever stained. His agony of contrite sorrow was commensurate with the enormity of his guilt; and the language of passionate grief and self-reproach is always hyperbolical. At such a moment, how naturally would his earliest sins, the sins of very infancy, like the ghosts of the long buried, have flashed upon his mental vision, and called forth vehement expressions of the deepest self-condemnation! And how natural an expression of those early sins are the words now under consideration, especially when we consider the highly impassioned style, in which the whole Psalm is written! There is no greater hyperbole in these words, viewed as referring to the sins of childhood and youth, than there is in the following words in the same connection: 'Purge me with hyssop, and I shall be clean: wash me, and I shall be whiter than snow. Make me to hear joy and gladness, that the bones which thou hast broken may rejoice.' We do not suppose that David's *bones* had actually been *broken*, or that

* Psalm li. 5.

he expected to be *whiter than snow;* why not then apply to the words under discussion the same rules of interpretation, which must confessedly be applied to these expressions? But, whatever is meant by these words, it is evident, beyond a shadow of doubt, that David did not write this Psalm as a careful, logical statement of doctrine, but merely as a humble, heart-stricken confession of sin before God. As such, it is to be read, interpreted, felt, and made profitable for reproof, and instruction in righteousness.

The other proof-text, to which I would make particular reference, is this: 'We all had our conversation in times past in the lust of our flesh, fulfilling the desire of the flesh and of the mind; and *were by nature children of wrath*, even as others.'* St. Paul is here addressing those recently converted from idolatry, and has spoken of their former sinful habits, which had subjected them to the divine displeasure. He adds: 'We Jews also led a similarly sinful life before our conversion, and were *by nature*, that is, *in our former condition*, as much the subjects of the divine displeasure, as much the children of wrath, as you were.' And the moral, which St. Paul deduces from this statement is, 'By grace are ye saved,' that is, Christian privileges came,

* Ephesians ii. 3.

not because you or we deserved them, but through the free, unpurchased mercy of God. The phrase, *by nature*, St. Paul elsewhere employs to denote *condition*, as, for instance, where he says: 'We who are Jews *by nature*, and not sinners of the Gentiles.*

But the Scriptural argument *against* the doctrine of native depravity, and in behalf of the rectitude of human nature, as it comes from the Creator's hand, is full, far beyond our need, and to the utmost limit of our desire.

In the first place, the almost numberless recognitions in the Bible, of man's moral accountability and of a future retribution, imply the native rectitude of human nature; for, in the precise proportion, in which human nature is depraved, man's accountability ceases, and he ceases to merit punishment for his sins.

Again, man is constantly addressed and treated in the Bible, as if he had within himself the means of forming a correct moral decision in many cases, though not the capacity to frame a perfect rule of conduct. Our Saviour asked the people: 'Why even of yourselves judge ye not what is right?' † He was in the constant habit of appealing to men's consciences, as if conscience had a real existence, and were always on the side of virtue. St. Paul speaks of the

* Galatians ii. 15. † Luke xii. 57.

Gentiles, who have not God's revealed law, as 'doing by nature the things contained in the law,' as 'being a law unto themselves,' and as 'shewing the work of the law written in their hearts,'* — all which is utterly inconsistent with the idea of native depravity.

Again, our Saviour speaks of little children, in a way, which shows that he saw no marks of depravity in them. When he wished to rebuke the unholy strife of his apostles, he 'called a little child unto him, and set him in the midst of them, and said, Verily, I say unto you, except ye be converted, and become as little children, ye shall not enter into the kingdom of heaven.' † When little children were brought, that he might bless them, instead of designating them as the children of perdition, and as lying under God's wrath and curse, he said, 'Of such is the kingdom of heaven.' ‡ These texts are with me decisive, as to *our Saviour's* opinion of human nature, and I desire to look no farther. I am sure that the nature, whose most recent and genuine representatives Christ pronounced nearest the kindom of heaven, must be a *good* nature, and worthy of its Maker and Father.

I might accumulate Scriptural proof indefinitely; but I have given you as much as you can need.

* Rom. ii. 14, 15. † Matt. xviii. 2, 3 ‡ Matt. xix. 14.

I have, in this lecture, occupied myself chiefly in exposing and combating a radically false view of human nature. But, while I would not abase, I would not inordinately glorify human nature. I believe it good and pure, yet frail. All man's appetites, impulses, powers, and innate sentiments, are good in themselves; and, fitly balanced, and employed in right directions and on worthy objects, must conduce to his own true good, and to the glory of his Maker. But let their balance be deranged, or let any of them be misdirected, they become ministers of sin and sources of evil. The bodily appetites are good in themselves, and, if confined to their lawful gratification, never interfere with man's virtue. The native emotions of the soul are all equally innocent; it is only excess or misdirection, that can make them sinful. The affections are the crown and joy of life; and, while fixed on worthy objects, are the unfailing means of pure happiness and vigorous spiritual growth. But human nature is composed of cravings, desires, and capacities, which must, at first, be nourished and directed through the agency of others, often through indiscreet, sometimes through wicked agency, and almost always through the blended agency of many, in which some faulty ingredients can hardly fail to mingle. Hence the sins of infancy and childhood; and the doctrine of native depravity ascribes to the Almighty's workmanship what is due to our rude, or weak, or foolish handling of it, — ascribes to nature what flows from education.

But the hour forbids my pursuing this train of remark; and I close by barely pointing out two important practical uses of the doctrine, which it has been the aim of this lecture to establish, namely, that God sends every human spirit into the world pure, free from all stain of sin, and endowed with no powers or affections, which are not good in themselves, and capable of a worthy and virtuous direction and development.

1. This view magnifies the evil of sin, and makes trangression against God a fit ground for the deepest self-reproach and the most hearty penitence. Did I believe that God had given me a sinful nature, I could not reproach myself for sin; for God would be the sinner; — I could not repent; for I should be conscious of no blame. But if God has made me upright, and I have sinned against the good and pure nature which he has given me, — if I have violated the laws of my own being, and made that, which he ordained for life, death, — then have I abundant reason for contrite sorrow. The sin is mine. I am not tempted of God. I can cast no reproach on the Author of my being. I must lay my hand upon my mouth, and my mouth in the dust, and cry, *unclean, unclean.*

2. The view, which regards human nature as

natively sinless and pure, cherishes humility. Did I believe myself utterly depraved by nature, I can hardly set limits to what my pride would be, on account of whatever slight and imperfect degree of virtue I might possess; for it would be so much raised from a barren and blighted soil. It would be a worthy ground for boasting. But if God has given me a nature perfectly adapted to his service, and capable of all things high and holy, and if I have, in ways and times without number, departed from the dictates of that nature, violated its laws, cramped or distorted its energies, neglected its culture, and suffered wild grapes to grow on the vine of God's careful planting and watchful husbandry, then must I feel humbled in view of what God has done and I have not done, of what he has given and I have not rendered back.

LECTURE VI.

REGENERATION.

JOHN III. 3.

EXCEPT A MAN BE BORN AGAIN, HE CANNOT SEE THE KINGDOM OF GOD.

THE connection, in which the conversation with Nicodemus occurs, casts so essential light upon the meaning of our text, that I will commence my discourse by calling your attention to it. Unfortunately, the arbitrary division of chapters breaks the thread of the narrative, which includes the last *three* verses of the *second* chapter,—'When Jesus was in Jerusalem in the feast day, many believed in his name, when they saw the miracles which he did,' that is, believed in him theoretically,—acknowledged him as a divine teacher, but without submitting their hearts and lives to his teachings. 'But Jesus did not commit himself unto them,'—did not repose entire trust in them,—did not admit them to a confidential footing; for he placed no value upon mere profession, or a mere barren belief.

'He knew all men,' read their characters, 'knew what was in man;' and bestowed or withheld his confidence accordingly. Under this general statement, to illustrate the mode in which Jesus dealt with those, to whom 'he did not commit himself,' the evangelist now brings forward the case of Nicodemus as an individual example. There was one of these intellectual, yet not spiritual converts, 'Nicodemus, a ruler of the Jews,' who for fear of losing caste among the Pharisees, 'came to Jesus by night,' no doubt with the purpose of securing his favor, whenever his star should be on the ascendant. He came with a profession of the belief, at which he had arrived on the feast-day: 'We know that thou art a teacher sent from God; for no man can do these miracles that thou doest, except God be with him.' Jesus, knowing what was in the man, and perceiving that his heart had not been touched by 'the word of the kingdom,' makes to him the declaration, which I have taken for my text: 'Except a man be born again, he cannot see the kingdom of God.' By this we must obviously understand our Saviour as saying to him: 'Nicodemus, it is not enough for thee to believe me a divine teacher, miraculously empowered and endowed. It is not enough for thee to be willing to follow me outwardly, when wealth and honor shall be in my train. Wouldst thou truly be my disciple, thou must be mine inwardly, in principle and character, — thou must be a different man, a new man, — thou must be born again.'

With regard to this passage, several erroneous views have been maintained. Some have supposed these words addressed to Nicodemus as a Jew, and have understood them as referring merely to the *change of opinion*, necessary in order for him to become a Christian. But, as we have seen, this change had already taken place, at least so far as it took place in the apostles during their Master's lifetime; for they ceased not to be devout Jews on account of their allegiance to Jesus. Nicodemus already believed Jesus to be a divine teacher. The change, which remained to be wrought in him, was that of principle and character.

It has been maintained by the Romish Church, and by many members of the English and American Episcopal Church, in whose service-book the idea is distinctly recognized, that *baptism*, even infant baptism, is the regeneration here spoken of; for, in amplifying his meaning, our Saviour says: 'Except a man be born of *water* and of the spirit, he cannot enter into the kingdom of God.' But, in my opinion, *water* in this verse does not even refer to *Christian* baptism; but to a form of baptism, with which Nicodemus was well acquainted. When the Jews received a proselyte into their fold, it was their custom to baptize, or wash with water, him and his whole family; and after this process, they were accustomed to call the proselyte *new-born*, or one *born again*. Now our Saviour introduces the *water* in this discourse, to signify to Nicodemus, that it was no such superficial process that he intended by the new birth, that a washing with water was not enough, and that something inward, not outward, must be wrought, in order to constitute true regeneration. 'Except a man be born, not merely of the water, which you deem enough to admit a man to the privileges of Judaism, but also of the divine spirit, he cannot enter into the kingdom of God.'

We have arrived, then, at the conclusion, that it is no mere change of opinions, nor yet a mere outward rite or profession, that is implied in being born again; but that the phrase denotes something inward and spiritual. Nicodemus stood, with reference to Christianity, precisely as the great mass of those born in Christian countries, and baptized in infancy, now stand, — in the attitude of intellectual belief, but not in that of moral obedience; nor is there any ground, on which the requisition of the new birth could have been made of Nicodemus, on which it should not also be made of every person of mature understanding, who is not already, in heart and life, a sincere and devoted follower of Christ. We are now prepared to answer the following questions, with reference to REGENERATION. What is regeneration? Is it essential to every human being? Is it instantaneous, or gradual? Is it an indelible process; or may the regenerate fall from their high estate? By what agency is it affected? What evidence of it in ourselves may we deem sufficient? What evidence of it should we seek in others, as a prerequisite to Christian fellowship?

I. *What is regeneration?* I hardly need tell you, that *regeneration* and *being born again* are synonymous,—the former being a word of Latin derivation, equivalent to the latter in Saxon English. The idea is that of a second birth. There are various orders of beings that are born twice. The butterfly is born at first a caterpillar, a mere earthworm, an unsightly, grovelling creature, without any apparent means of rising higher or becoming more beautiful. He is born again, a light, airy, beautiful being, with wings of gold and scarlet, the playmate of the zephyrs. Yet, when you examine his body, it is still the caterpillar, the earthworm, though etherealized,—the same shape, though endowed with an elasticity and beauty, to which before it was an utter stranger. And so likewise, in the caterpillar, there were the unseen rudiments of those beautiful wings,—the power, in its hidden germ, of that graceful flight. Thus his new birth is not a change, but a development, of his nature,

— not a new creation, but the putting forth of portions of his being, previously dormant. Man, too, in order to be what God means that he should be, must be born twice. For he is at first born merely an animal being, and a child of earth, — with powers, that fit him for a residence here, and the enjoyment of outward and earthly good, — with propensities, that dispose him to a grovelling life, without any aim beyond the present sphere of being. He is born indeed with spiritual capacities, but they are like the caterpillar's wings, at first unseen, folded, dormant; and, before they manifest themselves at all, the animal nature has acquired a decided, fearful preponderance and supremacy. Thus, when the spiritual nature at length begins to put forth, it generally finds itself overshadowed and dwarfed by the animal, so that it remains altogether subordinate, verifying, in him who has been born but once, the words of the wisdom of Solomon: 'The corruptible body presseth down the soul, and the earthly tabernacle weigheth down the mind that museth upon many things.' Therefore is it that a man must be born again, — born into the spiritual world, — born again, not by a change, but by a development of his nature, by the expanding of those wings of praise and prayer, that have remained folded and unused, by his entering upon a new sphere of being, and becoming a citizen of the unseen and spiritual world.

At the butterfly's first birth, his ethereal powers and tendencies are bound up, and crippled by the terrestrial. By his second birth, the ethereal element is put forth with sufficient vigor to buoy up and etherealize the terrestrial. In like manner, by virtue of man's first birth, the body weighs down and cramps the spiritual nature; but, by the second birth, the spiritual nature is drawn forth with an energy sufficient to subdue and spiritualize every bodily appetite and passion, and to make the body a willing servant of the soul. 'That which is born of the flesh is flesh,' earthly, sensual; 'that only which is born of the spirit, is spirit.' A spiritual state of the heart, of the affections, of the conduct, must be the result of a new and spiritual birth, just as an animal and earthly life is the result of the first birth of a human being into the outward world. As, by being born of the flesh, we bear the image of the earthly, so, by being born of the spirit, must we acquire the image of the heavenly. By our first birth, the animal nature has and keeps the supremacy; regeneration is the process, by which the spiritual nature acquires and retains the supremacy. By virtue of our first birth, we dwell upon the earth, and are adapted to it; by regeneration, we enter the kingdom of God, the spiritual world, and are fitted for its society, its duties, and its joys. By our first birth, we become heirs of the infirmities and ills of a mortal life; by regeneration, we acquire the powers and properties of an immortal being.

II. We next ask: *Is regeneration essential to every human being?* Can none but the regenerate enter the kingdom of God? Our very definition of regeneration answers this question sufficiently. 'Flesh and blood cannot inherit the kingdom of God.' For what is the kingdom of God? It is a society of all good and faithful spirits, bound together by the love and service of the Almighty. It is a kingdom, whose law is piety and duty, whose life is prayer and praise. It is a kingdom, where spiritual relations alone are recognized, where all dwell as children of God and brethren in Christ. Now it is absurd to maintain that man, any man, is born into this outward world, with powers, tastes, and habits, that fit him for such a society. It is absurd to maintain that any man can be fitted for this society, without a new development of powers and affections, on the full exercise of which he does not enter by virtue of his birth into the outward world.

The innocent child needs to be born again; for he brings into the world, not indeed a sinful nature, but a nature, whose better part unfolds not at once. And, in order for him to become fit for the kingdom of heaven, his spiritual nature must be developed and made supreme, which it is not in infancy, though it may be in early childhood. Perhaps in some instances, but seldom, regeneration is the result of education alone, so that the child's first choice is that of God, and duty, and spiritual pursuits and pleasures, and his character, from the earliest period of his moral agency, is a religious character. I say that this is probably the case but seldom, not because I think it intrinsically unnatural. On the other hand, I regard it as the natural result of such an education, as a child ought to have. But a thoroughly religious education has no doubt been exceedingly rare; for of religious parents, there are too many who give their children a worldly education; and, when parents do all that they ought and can, still they divide the education of their children with many persons and influences adverse to the spiritual life. For these reasons, most persons, if not all, live, for a longer or shorter period, a merely animal or worldly life, with little thought of spiritual things, with little taste for religious pursuits or enjoyments. And this life, however harmless, is a life of sin, because passed in the neglect of known duty. In this case, regeneration is a double process. It includes a pulling down, as well as a building up,—a death to sin, as well as a spiritual birth,—the putting off of the old man, as well as the putting on of the new man,

— the dethroning of flesh and sense, as well as the enthroning of God in the heart, — in fine, conversion, an entire change of character, a new heart, a new life. The infant needs to be regenerated, — you cannot say that he needs to be converted; for, if not probable, it is at least theoretically possible, that his regeneration may be effected by education alone. But in him, who has once willingly lived, for however short a season, a merely animal or worldly life, regeneration can take place only by means of conversion.

But how is it with those, who die too young to have formed religious characters? They, I reply, need regeneration, as much as if they had lived; for they have been for the most part obedient to mere bodily instincts, and they die with their spiritual natures undeveloped. They have, indeed, wrapped within their souls, the power of an angelic and immortal destiny; but it is folded and dormant, and needs, in order that they may be fit for heaven, to be expanded, and made quick, powerful, and supreme. But the infant dies sinless. He has no unholy desires, no evil habits, no unworthy loves, to make him wretched in the world whither he goes; and he goes where no fault, or error, or negligence in his education can render his regeneration doubtful, or make sin possible. He goes into the immediate presence of a Father, whose love must at once pervade and fill his unoccupied heart; for the innocent need only to know God, in order to love him. And the work of regeneration, which, in the world's imperfect school, it might have taken years to accomplish, may be the work of hours or moments in that higher school, where Jesus is the teacher.

But how is it with virtuous heathen, who have been faithful to the light that they have enjoyed, but have attained so inadequate views of duty and of divine truth, that their characters must needs fall very far short of that of the regenerate Christian? I answer, that, if they have governed their hearts and lives by the best rules of duty known to them, their regeneration has commenced,—they have acquired a love of duty, the habit of self-denial, a spiritual frame of mind, all which are traits of the regenerate character. They have the rectitude and singleness of purpose, the hunger and thirst after righteousness, requisite for their entrance into the Redeemer's fold. All that they need, to bring them to the stature of the perfect in Christ Jesus, is religious knowledge; and the body is the veil, which hides that knowledge from them. As soon as the veil is rent away, they behold their God and their Redeemer,—light bursts at once upon their disembodied spirits, completes their regeneration, and thus fits them for heaven.

But, not only those of preëminent lustre amidst surrounding darkness, not only those, whom we are accustomed to call the great and good men of heathenism, — many, very many others, I believe, will come from the east and the west, from the north and the south, and take their places among the children of the kingdom, — yes, literally among the *children* of the kingdom, in the place, on the footing of little children. While my own conscience tells me, that if I, and such as I, fail to clothe ourselves with all the graces of the regenerate heart, we shall be most righteously cast into the outer darkness, and, whatever we suffer, shall know and feel that God is just, I cannot believe that those, who, whether in heathen or in Christian lands, have not had the opportunity of religious culture, are all to forfeit heaven. No. I believe that God reveals some portion of his law to every rational being, however ignorant or degraded. I believe that there is some one thing, in which those altogether born in sin know their duty, that there is one talent committed even to the least privileged of the race, and that, if that one talent be improved, or that one duty discharged, the opportunity for complete regeneration, not vouchsafed to them on earth, may be afforded them in heaven. The keeping of the law in one point, if that one be the only point, on which the law is known, must make the soul willing and glad to keep the whole law, when the whole is revealed. Whereever, among the outcast and down-trodden on

Pagan or Christian soil, among those, who have had around them only depraved examples and corrupt influences, with not a ray of gospel light or a word of Christian teaching, — wherever, I say, among such, and in the midst of heart-sickening vice, there is a single beautiful trait of character, be it truth, or fidelity, or sympathy, or compassion, or benevolence, or a mere consciousness of degradation and misery, a vague, yet earnest longing for something purer and better, and a preparation of soul to hail the light if it should come,—such spirits, I believe, are among those to whom the Judge will say, not, 'Depart, ye cursed,' but, 'Come unto me, ye weary ones and heavy laden, and I will give you rest.' I believe that such spirits need only the light of heaven to regenerate them, while, for those who have buried or wasted either the one talent or the ten, there can be reserved only the doom of the wicked and slothful servant. Certainly there is, there must be in the judgment, a world-wide difference between those, to whom the Judge can say, 'Ye have both seen and hated both me and my Father,' and those, who had not the offer of salvation distinctly made to them, but who would have leaped with joy, had it reached them.

I should be sorry to think that I have a single hearer, so much a stranger to the love of God and the spirit of Christ, as to deem me a setter-forth of lax and dangerous doctrines, because I can, in deep and thankful sincerity, lay up a hope in heaven for those, to whom on earth no door of hope is opened. It is no lax doctrine for us. The law, that, where much is given, much will be required, but that, where little is bestowed, little will be demanded, is a law of uncompromising strictness and severity for you and me, who have known only the clear sunlight of gospel privilege. No one can place higher than I would, the responsibilities of those, who have the means of knowing Christ. But I earnestly protest against making the harsh and gloomy views, that one may take with regard to the unprivileged and benighted, a standard of piety. To the shame of Christians, this is often done; and I have known the piety of ministers of the gospel called in question, for no other reason, than that they maintained that the heathen would not be cast in a body into everlasting torments. I should be half disposed to hurl back the accusation, were it not written, 'Judge not, that ye be not judged;' for I cannot but feel that the man, who cherishes such sentiments, and myself, believe and worship two entirely different Gods.

III. We next inquire: *Is regeneration instantaneous, or gradual?* To man's eye, it must generally appear gradual; for the influences, which God commonly employs to convert the

16

soul, are gradual. Our Saviour also compares the growth of religion in the heart of man to the growth of grain, 'first the blade, then the ear, after that the full corn in the ear.' No doubt, many of what are called sudden conversions are gradual, (indeed, most of the cases of that kind, with which I have been conversant, have been so,) the particular event, or season of excitement, to which they are ascribed, being the occasion, rather than the cause of their development. In such cases, there has been a long series of unseen struggles, suppressed groanings, secret penitential regrets, heartfelt aspirations for holiness; and the religious character, which shoots up before man's sight with apparent suddenness, to the divine eye is the growth of months or years. The phenomena of such a conversion, (if we may compare joyful things with fearful,) might be likened to the eruption of a volcano, which, to the ignorant beholder, seems sudden, but to effect which, subterranean fires may have been burning for a century. But there are undoubtedly other cases, in which regeneration is really a very rapid process, — in which an immense amount of inward emotion and effort is crowded into an exceedingly brief period. God's convicting and converting spirit sometimes seems to fall like lightning from the heavens. We have seen those, who have professed, and seemed to come at once out of midnight darkness into

God's marvellous light. Yet, in most instances, and, as I cannot but think, in the most hopeful cases, the dawn first reddens, and the day-star rises, and the sky becomes bright and beautiful so gradually, that one can hardly say when night gives place to day.

In all cases, however, there is, doubtless, to the divine eye, a moment when the new birth takes place, when the scale turns, when the natural man loses, and the spiritual man gains the supremacy, when duty, piety, and heaven, assume the mastery over meaner passions and affections. The character always has for its index the ruling love, — the predominant aim, desire, or purpose, — the one master principle, which gives, as it were, the key-note to the whole life. Now a literal equipoise of the character, for more than a single moment, is hardly possible. The character must, at every moment of a man's existence, (even if the preponderance be slight,) be either worldly or spiritual; and, though a man may not be able to mark for himself the moment when the scale turns,—though, when he undertakes to determine it, he may antedate or postdate it,— yet it can hardly be otherwise than a moment distinctly marked by the divine eye.

IV. Our next question is: *Is regeneration an indelible process; or can those, who have been born again, so far fall back into sinful habits, as to forfeit the blessings of the Christian covenant?*

To this question I would reply, that the regenerate state is in itself a most hopeful one, and that it includes within itself great prospect and promise of perseverance, and even abundant reason to expect restoration from the first stages of declension and backsliding. The change of character, which it implies, is a truly momentous one. The heart is new; the life is new. The regenerate person has entered upon a new and attractive sphere of being, — has joined himself to a society, which can hardly fail to draw him constantly heavenward, — has commenced the discharge of duties, which are sanctifying in their very nature, — has begun to enjoy pleasures, which never cloy, but which sustain the constant desire to seek them yet again. The regenerate person has of course begun to lead a life of prayer; and there is abundant ground for the hope, that he, who has felt the comfort and joy of prayer, will not abandon it, and, while he still maintains the habit of prayer, he cannot fall back into a life of sin. The regenerate person has learned to look at objects, events, and his fellow beings, in their spiritual relations and aspects; and points of view once acquired we do not readily lose, so that there is strong hope that he, the eyes of whose understanding have once been opened, will not close them again. Above all, the regenerate person is the subject of peculiar aid and guidance from above, which will not be lightly or capriciously withdrawn, but can be forfeited only by long continued negligence. And, even when the regenerate person has once departed widely from the Christian covenant, or begun to wax cold and careless, he has, in his past experience of the blessedness of God's service, remembrances to smite him through with godly sorrow, and to call him back to the fold, from which he is wandering. There will be, in the recollection of times of perfect religious peace and reconciliation, a voice breathing the sentiment of our beautiful hymn: —

'What peaceful hours I once enjoyed!
How sweet their memory still!
But they have left an aching void
The world can never fill.'

And, stung with the memory of a peace once his, now shut out from his soul, there is hope that he will lift the cry: —

'Return, O holy Dove, return,
Sweet messenger of rest;
I hate the sins that made thee mourn,
And drove thee from my breast.

'The dearest idol I have known,
Whate'er that idol be,
Help me to tear it from thy throne,
And worship only thee.'

Thus true is the doctrine of *the perseverance of the saints* to our reasonable hope, with regard to those who have once been inwardly renewed. But this doctrine, as a positive, arbitrary, unbending dogma, without abatement or exception, is false, ensnaring, and dangerous. It is opposed to reason, experience, and Scripture; and, by creating a fatal consciousness of security, it does more than anything else can, to make itself false in individual cases. Very many fall, because they feel so sure that they can never fall. Very many continue in sin, because they know that they have once been regenerated, and they feel assured that, whatever they do, they cannot fail of heavenly blessedness. But there is nothing in the religious character to make it intrinsically ineffaceable. As it can be kept strong and growing only by *exercise unto godliness*, so it may be frittered away by lack of exercise.

Moreover, the Scriptures refer so often to the possibility of apostacy on the part of the regenerate, that it fills me with unfeigned surprise, that it should ever have been regarded as impossible, by any, who profess to take the Bible for their standard of doctrine. How constantly are the saints exhorted to steadfastness and perseverance, all which exhortations are foolish and absurd, if the saints cannot fall away. St. Paul could surely have no doubt of his own regeneration; and yet he speaks of his diligent self-discipline and mortification of the flesh,—'lest that by any means, when I have preached to others,

I myself should be a cast-away.'* St. Paul is addressing regenerate persons, when he says, 'Grieve not the holy spirit of God, whereby ye are sealed unto the day of redemption.'† The writer to the Hebrews, so far from saying that the regenerate cannot fall away, expressly speaks of the *impossibility* (by which we are to understand, I suppose, the extremest difficulty) *of renewing again unto repentance those who fall away*, after they have been 'once enlightened, and have tasted of the heavenly gift, and have been made partakers of the Holy Spirit, and have tasted of the good word of God, and the powers of the world to come.'‡

V. We now arrive at the question: *By what agency is regeneration effected?* By God's, or man's? I reply, by both. The true doctrine is implied in that text of St. Paul: 'Work out your own salvation with fear and trembling; for it is God that worketh in you both to will and to do of his good pleasure.'§ It used to be a mooted question in theology, whether God or man must take the first step in man's regeneration. But it is almost too foolish a question to discuss, and one, which a child ought to be able to answer from his first catechism. For has not God himself, by his own infinite mercy, forever

* 1 Corinthians ix. 27. † Ephesians iv. 30.
‡ Hebrews vi. 4–6. § Philippians ii. 12, 13.

barred out such an inquiry as this? Has he not drawn nigh to us, from the very dawn of our moral being, in the countless blessings and healing sorrows of his providence, — in the religious aspects and voices of nature, — in the teachings, warnings, promises of the gospel, — in the example, the love, the reconciling blood of Christ, — in secret visitings of his spirit, which we all have felt, which we cannot escape or shut out, and in which, in what countless instances, has he verified to each of our hearts the words, 'Behold, I stand at the door and knock!' Yes. And in every step that we take on the path to eternal life, is the Father with us, keeping our feet from falling, and our souls from death. We enter the outward world, and gain bodily strength and vigor, only because in him we live, and move, and have our being, — because he sustains this marvellous machine in tension and activity, keeps in tune the harp of thousand strings, supplies nature's waste from his own fountain of life, propels the warm current through every limb and every vein. Equally, it seems to me, does the soul's true life flow unceasingly from him. From him proceed all holy desires, good counsels, and just works. His working in us is the essential condition of our spiritual health and activity.

Yet, in regeneration, our will must consent with his. There must be a determined choice and effort on our part. The vows of penitence, the meditations on our Father's and our Saviour's love, the holy resolutions, the heavenward strivings, by which we are to be born again, must flow from our own free will and purpose; nor can we be inwardly renewed, without our own earnest and diligent effort, our own voluntary prayers, our own free-will offering, and cheerful, whole-hearted consecration of body, soul, and life to our Master's service. Aid from God we shall indeed have, and must have, at every step. It will be in the strength that he gives us, that we shall endure and conquer. But God's aid, essential and powerful as it is in the spiritual life, is not irresistible. God help us, as a judicious father helps a child, when he is unwilling to control, while he earnestly desires that he should decide and act rightly. Such a father gives his son kind advice, surrounds him with good examples and influences, furnishes him with the best materials of judgment; but still the son may, from waywardness or passion, decide and act contrary to the father's wishes. Of this nature are the influences of the Divine Spirit for man's regeneration,—influences, which may be grieved and quenched, or which may be made to bring forth fruit unto everlasting life.

VI. We next ask: *What evidences of regeneration in ourselves ought we to deem sufficient?* This question it is the object of so much of my preaching to answer, that I the less regret the narrow space, in which it must be answered now. In general terms, *spirituality of character* is the sign that we have been born again. 'That which is born of the spirit, is spirit. If we are regenerated, we shall look at things in their spiritual aspects; and shall regard our spiritual relations and duties as of paramount importance. We shall delight in prayer. We shall habitually feel the presence of God, and shall refer our thoughts, words, and deeds, to his will and law, as to their only standard. Religious subjects, duties, and services, will always be welcome, and never a weariness or a burden. But the supreme law of the spiritual life is *love*,—love to God,—love to every child of God,—love to God with the heart and soul, the mind and strength,—love to man, tender, constant, forbearing, forgiving, ready to impart, glad to bless, rejoicing with the happy, sympathizing with the afflicted, showing mercy to all.

In the regenerate life, also, we are united to Christ, as the branch to the vine. Our virtues grow from his. Our spiritual graces twine themselves about him as their tree of life. There is a conscious reception of light and aid from his example and his spirit. We shall be able to say of this sin, 'I have striven against it, because my Master forbade it;' and of that virtue, 'I have labored to acquire it, because I found it in the Lord Jesus;' and of our general tone of character and habits of life, 'I am what I am, because I have been with Jesus, and learned of him, and humbly striven to follow him in all things.'

These hints may supply heads of self-examination, which I have not time to draw out as I could wish; and they must needs recall to my stated hearers the tests of Christian character, which they are wont to hear set forth from this pulpit.

VII. I hasten to our closing inquiry: *What evidence of regeneration should we seek in others, as a prerequisite to Christian fellowship?* None but the all-seeing God can tell with certainty, who are the regenerate, and who the unsanctified. In the Christian Church, the wheat and the tares must grow together till the harvest. Therefore, while, in judging of our own spiritual state, we should make our standard of Christian character as high as possible, in determining with whom we will hold Christian fellowship, we should so shape it, as to include even 'the least in the kingdom of heaven.' By making our terms of fellowship thus broad, we may indeed embrace some, whose names are not written in the book of life; but we had better treat as Christian brethren ten false pretenders to the name, than reject one, whom Christ has received.

Let us beware how we make our own creed, or ritual, or views of duty on any points that admit of question, a standard for our brethren. On these points we are as liable to err as they are; and they have the same right to condemn us, that we have to condemn them. But there are two things, which we may expect to find in the subjects of Christian regeneration, and the lack of either of which would compel us, however reluctantly, to doubt the Christian character of one, who on any ground sought to be recognized as a Christian. One of these relates to profession; the other to practice.

1. The *first* is a willingness to own Christ as an authoritative teacher, and as the one appointed Mediator between God and man, and, as a consequence of this, habitual reverence for his name, his gospel, and everything that he has made sacred. Christian fellowship is a fellowship in Christ, and not out of him. If, therefore, he be disowned, his name blasphemed, and his gospel set at nought, by any men of virtuous life and conversation, we may and should give them full credit for whatever virtues they manifest, and whatever good they do; but it is absurd to think of them as subjects for Christian fellowship. Were we, on account of their good lives, to call them Christians, we should be conferring a name, which is not ours to give, but can be given only to those, for whom it is appointed

by the Father; and he surely cannot have appointed it for any, by whom it is despised or undervalued.

2. The other essential prerequisite to Christian recognition, is a general outward conformity to the unquestioned rules of duty; — a generally virtuous life and conversation. We are not to look for perfection in others, while we are conscious of falling far short of it ourselves. But we may expect in those, who are renewed through the grace of Christ, some good degree of conformity to his image and spirit.

But, after all, the best rule is, for us to be as close and thorough as we can be, in the judgment of our own hearts; but always to bring to the judgment of another's character that charity, which 'thinketh no evil, believeth all things, and hopeth all things.'

I trust that this discussion, though in the form of a doctrinal exposition, may not pass, without leading my hearers to diligent self-examination as to the momentous question of their own regeneration. Of this question, my friends, nothing can take precedence. The time is hastening on for each of us, and for some is doubtless near, when it will be echoed in the thunder tones of approaching death. Let it be put and answered by each of us before he sleeps; and, whatever our amiable traits of character, whatever our endowments of mind and heart, if not sanctified by Christian faith and the spirit of self-consecration, let us hear, as from the lips of him, whose words are God's eternal truth, 'Except a man be born again, he cannot see the kingdom of God.'

LECTURE VII.

THE ATONEMENT.

2 CORINTHIANS V. 18, 19.

THE MINISTRY OF RECONCILIATION, TO WIT, THAT GOD WAS IN CHRIST RECONCILING THE WORLD UNTO HIMSELF.

THE ATONEMENT will be the subject of the two remaining lectures of this course. I commence with a few remarks on the word *atonement*, and its use in the Scriptures. *Atonement* is *at-one-ment*, reconciliation, the bringing together, or *at one*, of those who have been at variance. It is a word employed but once in our translation of the New Testament; and that is in the following passage: 'If, when we were enemies, we were reconciled to God by the death of his Son, much more, being reconciled, we shall be saved by his life. And not only so, but we also joy in God, through our Lord Jesus Christ, by whom we have now received the *atonement*,' that is, the *reconciliation* just spoken of.* The same Greek

* Romans v. 10, 11.

word occurs elsewhere, but is rendered *reconciliation.* It is the word so rendered in our text. The word *atonement* is often used in our translation of the Old Testament; but there it simply means *ritual purification*, and can have no reference to reconciliation between God and man, since atonement is said to have been made for inanimate objects, as for the altar, and for a house infected with leprosy. The Hebrew word rendered to *atone*, denotes to *cover*, or *smear over;* and it no doubt came to imply *purification*, from the ceremonial *smearing* of the persons or things purified, with oil or with blood.

Atonement, reconciliation between God and man, through Christ, through his death, is the doctrine of all Christian believers. The question at issue is, Which party did Christ reconcile to the other,—God to man, or man to God? Some suppose that Christ died to reconcile God to man, to appease the divine wrath, to make God willing or able to forgive man's guilt. Others maintain that God never was, and never can be alienated from his human family, so as to need atonement; but that it is man, alienated from God by sin, that needs and receives the atonement, and that Christ lived and died to reconcile guilty man to a Father of unchangeable love. The latter is the view, which you have always heard from this pulpit. The former is the theory of that branch of the Church called Calvinistic.

The Calvinistic doctrine, stated more in detail, is this. God has affixed to every sin, nay, to original sin derived from Adam, the penalty of eternal torments. God's justice forbids him to forgive man's iniquity, unless this penalty be in some way satisfied. Christ interposed, and took upon himself the weight of agony and torment, which those who are forgiven would otherwise have borne, and because he thus suffered in their stead, they go clear. This doctrine, with slight modifications, is held by the majority of our Christian public. One of these modifications introduces the idea of imputed righteousness, maintaining that, as men, though personally guiltless, are made sinners by the imputation of Adam's guilt, so those, who are saved, though personally destitute of holiness, are made holy by the righteousness of Christ imputed to them. This is a notion so opposed to common sense, so self-contradictory in its terms, and so generally laid aside by its former advocates, as to claim only the most cursory notice. Another modification of the popular doctrine is, that, though Christ may not have suffered the full amount of what was due to man's guilt, yet what he suffered was accepted by the Father as a full equivalent for what man ought to have suffered. But the main idea of this doctrine, in all its modifications, is *substitution*, *vicariousness*, one's standing in another's stead, and bearing what he ought to have borne.

The first remark to be made upon this doctrine is, that it is nowhere distinctly stated in the Scriptures. This its advocates admit. They maintain that it is strongly implied in several scattered texts in the apostolic epistles, and in one or two in the prophet Isaiah. But is it conceivable that a doctrine of such infinite moment should not have been explicitly stated in the Bible? It is, I think, admitted on all sides, that a vicarious atonement was not distinctly taught by our Saviour in any of his recorded discourses, and that, when he died, his immediate followers were as ignorant of the purpose of his death, as they were at his nativity. But why was this? He often spoke of his approaching dissolution; why did he make no disclosure of its purpose? By the statements, which he did make, he manifestly failed to reconcile his disciples to his departure from them; but, had he once told them that God could not pardon the penitent without his dying, they would have understood that it was expedient for them that he should go away. Nor yet does our Saviour make any additional disclosure on this point after his resurrection.

The vicarious atonement, one would suppose, must have formed, if true, an essential part of the preaching of the apostles. But, in the discourses preached by Peter and Paul to congregations, that were listening to Christian instruction for the first time, we find not a word of this doctrine, now regarded by so many as the cardinal point of the gospel scheme. Yet, through these discourses, converts were made by thousands; and these, not converts of an hour, but such as 'continued steadfastly in the apostles' doctrine and fellowship.'

Equally little do we find of this doctrine in the writings of the Christian fathers of the first three centuries. The idea of substitution, or of a price paid to appease the divine justice, cannot be traced in any of their works now extant, though among these works are creeds, defences, apologies, and avowed statements of the whole Christian system. This fact is admitted, and referred to with surprise, by Orthodox commentators upon the writings of the fathers. Flacius, a learned pupil of Luther, says that the Christian writers of the primitive age 'discoursed, like philosophers, of the law, and its moral precepts, and of the nature of virtue and vice; but they were totally ignorant of man's natural corruption, the mysteries of the gospel, and Christ's merits.' The same writer, speaking of Eusebius, the ecclesiastical historian, (who flourished early in the fourth century, and than whom none stood higher in the Church on the score of learning or authority,) says: 'It is a very low and imperfect description, which he gives of a Christian, making him *only* a man, who, by the knowledge of Christ and his doctrine, is brought to the worship of the one true God, and the practice of sobriety, righteousness, patience, and other virtues. But he has not a word about imputed righteousness.' I cannot forbear quoting the well-merited and delicate irony, with which Lardner dismisses these passages from Flacius. 'Poor, ignorant, primitive Christians, I wonder how they could find the way to heaven. They lived near the time of Christ and his apostles. They highly valued, and diligently read the Holy Scriptures, and some of them wrote commentaries upon them; but yet, it seems they knew little or nothing of their religion, though they embraced and professed it with the manifest hazard of all earthly good things; and many of them laid down their lives, rather than renounce it.'

These considerations certainly furnish a strong presumption against the doctrine under discussion, yet cannot be regarded as conclusive; for they have been admitted by its most intelligent advocates and defenders. Let us then analyze the doctrine, and see on what foundation it rests.

It assumes for its basis the position, that God's law annexes eternal punishment to every sin, without reference to the repentance or reformation of the sinner. This is an idea wholly unsustained by Scripture, and supported mainly by fragments of texts, which, quoted entire, would imply the opposite doctrine. It is stated as the stern, unbending law of God's revealed word, 'The soul that sinneth, it shall die.' This is indeed a part of the law as revealed through Ezekiel. But the prophet adds: 'But if the wicked will turn from all his sins that he hath committed, and keep all my statutes, and do that which is lawful and right, he shall surely live, he shall not die. All his transgressions that he hath committed, they shall not be mentioned unto him: in his righteousness that he hath done he shall live. Have I any pleasure at all that the wicked should die? saith the Lord God: and not that he should return from his ways, and live?'* Now I am utterly unable to discern the propriety, or the honesty of quoting the first portion of this passage, as the eternal moral law of God, and omitting the latter part. All through the Old Testament, the promise of pardon to the penitent is connected with the denunciation of punishment against the sinner. 'If they shall confess their iniquity, then will I remember my covenant,' was God's uniform declaration to the nation of Israel. The whole spirit of the Old Testament towards sinners is expressed in these words of God through Ezekiel: 'When I say unto the wicked, Thou shalt surely die; if he

* Ezekiel xviii. 20-23.

turn from his sin, and do that which is lawful and right; if the wicked restore the pledge, give again that he had robbed, walk in the statutes of life, without committing iniquity: he shall surely live, he shall not die.'* It is said that this law of pardon had reference to the intended sacrifice of Christ,—to 'the Lamb slain from the foundation of the world?' This is an entirely gratuitous assumption, not only unsustained by Scripture, but opposed to certain very plain declarations of the New Testament, which represent Christ's mission as *the consequence*, not the cause, *of God's forgiving mercy.* Such are these texts, which might be multiplied indefinitely. '*God so loved the world that he gave his only begotten Son*, that whosoever believeth in him, should not perish, but have everlasting life.'† 'Herein is love, not that we loved God, but that *he loved us, and sent his Son* to be the propitiation for our sins.'‡ '*God was in Christ, reconciling the world unto himself.*' §

But it is maintained that divine justice forbids the pardon of the penitent. Now, by *justice* as applied to God, we either mean some attribute, of which we have no knowledge, or else we mean the same attribute, which we denominate *justice* between man and man. If the former, then whatever we affirm or deny with regard to

* Ezekiel xxxiii. 14, 15.
† John iii. 16.
‡ 1 John iv. 10.
§ 2 Corinthians v. 19.

the divine justice is mere hap-hazard assertion, and one assertion is as good as another. But to my mind nothing is more certain than this,—that, when God reveals himself to mankind as *merciful*, and *holy*, and *just*, he means, that he is possessed of those attributes, which all men designate, and which good men cherish and practice, as *mercy*, *holiness*, and *justice*. Now let me put the question to your hearts and consciences, is it unjust to forgive the wrong-doer, when he repents? If my neighbor has done me a very great injury, and now repents of it, is it unjust for me to forgive him? You would think me beside myself, were I to ask the question seriously, and with regard to a case actually in hand. In forgiving my penitent neighbor, I wrong no one. I give him what I take from no one else; for mercy grows by exercise. I give him what I owe him as a fellow-being, and a legitimate object of sympathy and charity. If your little child has been disobedient, and is now sorry for it, do you regard it as unjust for you to forgive him? Are you unrighteous, because, on account of his regret for his fault and his promise of amendment, you forbear the chastisement, which the fault persisted in might seem to merit? No; for you only give to the child from that fountain of paternal love, which God caused to well up within you for the child's benefit. You give the child what is rightfully his own. No more is

God unjust in extending free, unpurchased mercy to his penitent child.

Still farther, I contend that divine justice not only admits, but necessarily includes and implies, the forgiveness of the penitent sinner. It would be unjust for God not to forgive the contrite. That stern, flinty, inexorable *vice*, not virtue, which technical theologians have been wont to call *justice*, is not what they term it. Such a counterfeit of justice, if it exist anywhere, is to be found with the devil and his angels. True justice is the perfection of goodness. It is a goodness, which does no wrong, which is impartial, and not a respecter of persons, which renders to all their due, and which, in every place and relation, discharges the appropriate offices of that place or relation. Now God is our Father; and the justice of a father is firm, discreet, impartial, yet munificent affection. What title to the character of a just man could be claimed, think you, by that human father, who turned a deaf ear to the sincere penitence of his erring son? To be sure, the son could base no claim upon his past merits. But the father would owe it to his own nature, to the spontaneous impulses of a paternal heart, to forgive him. He would do himself the most outrageous injustice by persevering in anger and in vindictive measures. Thus it is also with our Father in heaven. Though his erring children can build no claim on the ground of past merit or obedience, he yet owes to himself to forgive them. He would be unjust, false to his own nature, were he to despise the sighing of the contrite, and the desire of the penitent. He would, in that case, withhold from men that, which, though they could not claim it on the score of merit, is their rightful due as his creatures, as his children. I maintain, then, that the forgiveness of the sincere penitent is an essential part of the divine justice. As such it is represented by the sacred writers. What could be more explicit on this point, than St. John's declaration: 'If we confess our sins, God is *faithful and just* to forgive us our sins?'*

I next remark, that, if it is inconsistent with the divine justice not to forgive the penitent, it is still more so, to punish the innocent instead of the guilty. If justice has any signification whatever, it certainly includes and implies the rendering to each individual, and to no other in his stead or for his sake, the good or the evil that is his due. Apply the principle of the vicarious atonement to human affairs, and see how much wrong it would produce, of how much iniquity it would be the parent. We will suppose a case. A man has been sentenced to the penitentiary for forgery, for a term of *twenty* years. At the expiration of *ten* years, it is represented to the chief magistrate, that, at an early period of his

* 1 John i. 9.

confinement, he showed decided marks of deep contrition, that his conduct has been without exception exemplary, and that he will, undoubtedly, if pardoned, be a worthy and valuable member of society, in fine, that he is among the fittest subjects for executive clemency. The governor says: 'Yes, he surely ought to be pardoned. But the sentence must be executed. Go then, take him from his cell, and immure in his stead, for the next *ten* years, that good man over the way. He has never broken the law in any one point. He is the best citizen we have; and there is no other man, by whose imprisonment the majesty of the law can be so well sustained.' Would you not infer, that this magistrate's conscience and moral sentiment had been paralyzed? Would you not deem such a procedure the very climax of unrighteousness? Or suppose that one of my children had incurred some threatened punishment, but was now penitent for the fault, and that the other, an innocent, loving little creature, begged to be punished in her sister's stead, — you would never afterwards trust my judgment in matters of right and wrong, if, even at the instance of the child's own compassion, I punished the faultless one, and let the guilty go. The native instinct of the human heart relucts at the very idea of a vicarious penalty, and demands that punishment be either remitted, or visited upon the offender in his own person. Now it is in the highest degree unbecoming and irreverent to ascribe to God a course of conduct, which we should reprehend and despise in man.

But it is said, that to forgive the sin of the penitent, without laying its punishment on some other person, encourages sin. I have never been able to see the force of this objection to the doctrine of the free, unpurchased mercy of God. And, if it has any force, it belongs no less to the doctrine of vicarious atonement, than to that of free pardon; for, in either case, repentance is the only condition required of the sinner. Nor can he be restrained from sin by an unwillingness to add to the sufferings of his substitute; for, according to the popular doctrine, the punishment, and that an infinite one, has been already borne, and consequently cannot be increased by any additional amount of guilt. To my mind, forgiveness on the sole condition of repentance holds out a premium to goodness, not to sin. It keeps the prize of holiness within sight and reach of the sinner at every pause of his guilty career, whenever conscience wakes and passion sleeps. It opens, from every corner in his path of sin, cross paths to the road, from which he has wandered. It cries at every step, 'Turn ye, turn ye; for why will ye die?' It seems to me to imply the strangest confusion of ideas, to maintain that sin is encouraged by promises, which can be of no effect, till sin is repented of and forsaken.

But we are told, that the burdened conscience needs a vicarious atonement, and can feel secure of forgiveness, only when it can behold its punishment laid upon another's shoulders. That this feeling is a very frequent element in religious experience, I have no doubt. I believe that very many burdened consciences can find relief only through a vicarious atonement. But this state of feeling is created by the very doctrine, which it craves. Men feel thus, when under conviction of sin, because they have been taught to regard the Almighty as unwilling or unable to forgive sin, without the substituted suffering of another, — because they have never had the infinite mercy of God presented to them as a ground of trust and hope, — because they have always had associations of wrath and vengeance connected with him, and thus have been constrained to look to the Son for that forgiveness, for which they have been forbidden to go to the Father. But, where the Father's forgiving love is set forth as full, large, and free, the sin-burdened conscience can cast its burden upon him, though in utter self-reproach and self-abasement, yet without a shadow of doubt or fear.

I have thus far reasoned, as if the popular dogma of the atonement were consistent with the confessedly Scriptural doctrine of the remission or forgiveness of sins. But it is not so. If the one be true, the other cannot be. If you owe me a sum of money, and your neighbor pays it to me in your stead, there is no remission of the debt on my part. If you injure me, and I punish your son or brother in your stead, I exercise no forgiveness. Vicarious punishment is not pardon; but the two are at opposite poles of the moral universe. If God has taken full punishment upon Christ, if he has exacted from him the full price, he has put it for ever out of his own power to forgive sin, — he has blotted the very idea of pardon out of his book, — he has made the remission of sin, impossible. If Christ has paid my debt, I owe nothing. If Christ has borne my punishment, I am no longer liable to punishment. I therefore can no longer be the subject of pardon, or of the remission of sins. But if there is any one doctrine, that gives the key-note to the whole New Testament, it is that of the forgiveness of sins; and the dogma, which renders this impossible, can have no place in the counsel of God.

We might, were it necessary, show the absurdity of the popular notion of the vicariousness of Christ's sufferings, by a still farther analysis of the ideas, which it includes or implies. It is a doctrine held only by Trinitarians; and to them the question may be fairly put, How can God punish God, or be punished by God? How can God pay a penalty to God, or cancel a debt due to God? This difficulty was felt by some of the early advocates of the doctrine under consideration; and, to obviate it, they decided, (and such was the general belief of the church for several centuries,) that the price or penalty, paid by Christ, was paid to the devil, in lieu of the souls which Christ ransomed from his power.

We might also ask, how is it in the nature of things possible, that Christ, an innocent, holy being, could have borne the punishment due to human guilt? For in what does that punishment consist? It consists in the forfeiture of the divine favor, and of the sympathy and com panionship of the good, in the stings of an evil conscience, in the undying goadings of depraved desire and unholy passion, in a state of protracted opposition to the divine government and disobedience of the divine law. It is a burden, which, from its very nature, could have been borne by no innocent being, least of all, by a being perfect, divine, and infinite.

It is said, that, in intense physical suffering, Christ bore the *full equivalent* of these inward torments due to the sins of the whole world? We ask, when; where? We read, indeed, of the agony of Gethsemane. But that, though intense and awful, was but for a brief season, and was sustained with a spirit so full of submission and of filial piety, as to make such woe, even if protracted through eternity, a heaven, compared with the torment of an unreconciled and rebellious soul. Then, at the crucifixion, there was the one exclamation, 'My God, my God, why hast thou forsaken me?' This, there is indeed some reason to suppose, was designed simply as a citation of the psalm commencing with these words, which contains many things applicable to Jesus. But if, (as seems to me more probable,) this exclamation was an expression of the feeling of the moment, it cannot have implied, that he deemed himself deserted by him, to whom, a moment afterwards, he said in the calm confidence of a child, 'Father, into thy hands I commend my spirit;' but it must have had reference to those outward circumstances of tribulation, which we are accustomed to call the *hidings of God's countenance*, so that it must be understood to mean, 'My God, why hast thou, in thine inscrutable wisdom, seen fit to leave me under such a weight of torture and of contumely?' But, with the exception of the agony in Gethsemane, and the inference that might be drawn, (wrongly, as I think,) from that momentary exclamation on the cross, the whole scene of the betrayal and crucifixion is so far from presenting the picture of one, who was enduring the eternal suffering of myriads compressed into a few hours, that it gives us rather the idea of a victory over suffering and death, so entirely won before the hour came, as to leave our Saviour's spirit, with but a passing cloud, calm, free, unburdened, elastic, full of heavenly communings, and consciously in the bosom of the Father. But, supposing the popular doctrine of Christ's vicarious suffering true, could such an inconceivable weight of anguish have been laid upon him, without having left, in the record of those hours, traces of an agony so unearthly, so infinitely surpassing the previous imagination of beholders, that the cry of the suffering God-man would have thrilled through the universe, and the horror and despair of the appalling scene would have seemed like the opening of the bottomless pit, beneath the feet of those that stood by? What! A thousand times ten thousand, nay, uncounted millions of eternal, and therefore infinite, burdens of the most intense and hopeless torment of body and soul, and all these laid upon Christ's human nature, which is represented as finite, — is there any trace, or shadowing forth of this, anywhere in the sacred history? Calvin, perceiving this difficulty, maintained that Christ spent the interval between his death and his resurrection in hell, suffering there the utmost possible measure of torment and agony; and, if the doctrine of a vicarious atonement be true, this supposition is indispensably necessary, to reconcile it with the narrative of the evangelists.

We might also argue against the idea of a vicarious atonement from its manifest inconsistency with every statement of doctrine or duty, with every discourse or parable in the New Testament, which is capable of being considered in connection with it. Take, for instance, the parable of the master, whose servant owed him a thousand talents, — a parable, which was expressly designed to illustrate the divine forgiveness, and which we cannot suppose the great Teacher to have so framed, as to exclude the essential conditions of forgiveness. Insert in this parable the vicarious atonement, — suppose the master to exact full payment of some other servant, — what a heartless mockery do you make of the words, 'He freely forgave him the debt!'

To take another instance, the parable of the prodigal son was undoubtedly designed to exhibit God's mercy to the penitent. Insert in this the idea of vicarious punishment. Suppose the parable to read as follows, (and such must be its actual import, if the doctrine under discussion be true.) 'And when the Father saw the wanderer returning with every mark of contrite sorrow, he called the elder son, who had always served him, nor transgressed at any time his commandments, and said, My son, my first-born and best beloved, here is thy lost brother coming back again, and begging for the bread of my house; but the word has gone forth from my lips, that the child, who once leaves my house, shall never return; and I know not how to remit this sentence, unless thou wilt take upon thyself the shame, and woe, and suffering due to his waywardness.' Who does not perceive, that, with this gloss, the parable loses all its worth and beauty? Nay, had it been thus written, instead of being oftener read, and more attractive, than any other portion of the Bible, it would have been almost repulsive enough, to have sunk into neglect and oblivion the gospel that contained it.

I might refer you, in this connection, to the petition in our Lord's prayer, 'Forgive our debts, as we forgive our debtors.' One, who believes in the vicarious sufferings of Christ, cannot use this petition with sincerity; for he hopes to be forgiven in a very different way from that, in which he knows it to be his duty to forgive. God's forgiveness is often held forth in the New Testament, as a measure and an example for man's forgiveness. Upon what an appalling career of wrong and crime should we enter, were we to make God's forgiveness on account of the substituted sufferings of the innocent, the measure and example for our own!

I next remark, that the doctrine of Christ's vicarious suffering represents God as a changeable being,—as indisposed at first to show mercy, but made placable by the death of Christ. Take, for instance, the sentiment of one of Dr. Watts's hymns, much used in our Calvinistic churches, in which, speaking of God's throne, he employs the following terrific language: —

'Once 'twas a seat of dreadful wrath,
  And shot devouring flame;
Our God appear'd consuming fire,
  And vengeance was his name.

'Rich were the drops of Jesus' blood,
  That calm'd his frowning face,
That sprinkled o'er the burning throne,
  And turned the wrath to grace.'

Oh, when I have heard these words read or sung, the image, that they have brought to my mind, has been the farthest possible from that of the Father God, of whom Jesus said, 'He so loved the world that he sent his Son.' They have, on the other hand, placed before me the semblance of a blood-thirsty fiend, at first ravening for his prey, and to be approached with safety, only when satiated with carnage. But has he, whose words are, 'I am Jehovah, I change not,' indeed sustained such an entire revolution of disposition and character? So says the theology of the schools. So says not the New Testament, which never represents Christ's mission and death as the cause of the Father's love, but always as its fruit and pledge. Indeed, it is to my mind a conclusive argument against a vicarious atonement, that, wherever, in the

New Testament, God is named in connection with the mediation and death of Christ, he is spoken of, not as the *object* of Christ's mission and atonement, but as its *author*, and as having originated it in love to men, that he might draw them to himself.

But it is urged by the advocates of the popular doctrine, that Christ's death is often spoken of in the Scriptures as a *sacrifice*. This is indeed the case; and I know of no term, which could have been more naturally and properly applied to the death of Christ, than this. His death was a sacrifice offered for the redemption of man. This, no Christian doubts. The question is, was it a *vicarious* sacrifice? That it was not, would appear from the striking, yet neglected fact, that, in the Scriptures, *Christ is oftener compared to a sacrifice, which was not even a sin-offering, namely, to the paschal lamb, than to any other part of the Jewish ritual.* He is frequently called *the Lamb*, also *our passover*. The figure is drawn out in full by St. Paul in the following text: 'Christ our passover is sacrificed for us; therefore let us keep the feast, not with the old leaven, neither with the leaven of malice and wickedness; but with the unleavened bread of sincerity and truth.'* The passover was a commemorative festival, by which the Hebrews cele-

* 1 Corinthians v. 7, 8.

brated their deliverance from Egyptian bondage; and the paschal lamb was the chief food for this anniversary supper. Christ in his death was likened to this lamb, because there clustered about his death associations of deliverance from a worse than Egyptian bondage, from the slavery of doubt, and fear, and sin; and also, because, in the Christian festival, designed to supersede the passover, bread, emblematic of the Saviour's body broken on the cross, took the place of the paschal lamb.

The vicarious atonement has been professedly sustained by analogies drawn from the Old Testament; but, in point of fact, there was no such thing as vicarious suffering under the Jewish law. Most of the Jewish offerings and sacrifices were not sin-offerings; but either thank-offerings, offerings of firstlings and first-fruits, designed chiefly for the subsistence of the priests and Levites; or offerings in acknowledgment, as those unintended omissions or transgressions of the ritual law, to which no moral guilt was attached. Moreover, very many of the sacrifices were bloodless ones, offerings of fine flour, oil, wine, fruit, and grain. And in this connection, it is an important and instructive fact, that the animal, made typically to bear the sins of the whole people, on the great annual day of atonement, was not slain. 'The priest shall lay both his hands upon the head of the goat, and confess over him all the iniquities of the children of Israel, and all their transgressions in all their sins, putting them upon the head of the goat; and shall send him away by the hand of a fit man into the wilderness: and the goat shall bear upon him all their iniquities unto a land not inhabited: and he shall let go the goat in the wilderness.'* This is the only instance in the Old Testament, in which sin is said to be laid upon any animal, or in which language seeming to imply vicariousness or substitution is used in connection with any part of the Mosaic ritual; and, in this service, the animal was not made to suffer in any form or way. But this was a part of the great annual confession-service or remission-service, in which, if anywhere, the idea of vicarious suffering must needs have been introduced. This idea, however, cannot be traced in any portion or feature of the Mosaic dispensation.

Sacrifice was, in fact, a symbolical form of worship, which all nations have practised in their infancy, and which, under the Mosaic law, was regulated and sanctioned, as still adapted to the imperfect culture and rude habits of the covenant people. Under a low state of civilization, sacrifice was an obvious means of attesting the sincerity of the religious sentiment. It was symbolical prayer or praise. He, who was penitent,

* Leviticus xvi. 21, 22.

fined himself in a sin-offering. He, who was thankful, showed the fervor of his gratitude by setting aside from his own use, and consecrating in some form, accordant with the notions of his times, a part of that wherein God had prospered him. Christ's death bore, therefore, a closer analogy to the slaying of the paschal lamb, with its glad associations of deliverance and divine guidance, than to any other part of the ancient ritual; and we can thus account for the frequency with which the passover furnishes the sacred writers with the phraseology employed with reference to the crucifixion.

Inasmuch as Christ's death was a sacrifice, whatever view we may take of its object or its efficacy, it would have been very strange if the sacred writers, who were all Jews, had not often employed with reference to it the word *sacrifice*, and the phrases usually connected with that word. But it would have been still more strange, and certainly would have authorized the suspicion of some peculiar and mysterious signification attached to this phraseology, if, employing it with reference to the death of Christ, they had used it on no other subject. But such is not the case. They have used the word *sacrifice* (and connected with it *offer up* and similar phrases) with reference to a large variety of subjects. The following are a few of the instances. 'I beseech you, therefore, brethren, that ye present your bodies a living sacrifice.'* 'If I be offered upon the sacrifice and service of your faith, I joy, and rejoice with you all.'† 'I am full, having received of Epaphroditus the things which were sent from you, an odor of a sweet smell, a sacrifice acceptable, well-pleasing to God.'‡ 'Let us offer the sacrifice of praise to God continually, that is, the fruit of our lips, giving thanks to his name. But to do good, and to communicate, forget not; for with such sacrifices God is well pleased.'§ 'Ye also, as lively stones, are built up a spiritual house, an holy priesthood, to offer up spiritual sacrifices, acceptable to God by Jesus Christ.'|| From these examples, we see that nothing like vicarious suffering is implied in the frequent comparison of our Saviour's death to the sacrifices under the Jewish ritual.

Indeed, would we only interpret the sacred writings by the common laws and customs of speech, we should be at no loss for the origin of phraseology of the kind now under consideration. In figurative language, we constantly style beings, whether human or divine, whom we revere or love, by the names of objects which we peculiarly admire or prize. How frequently are such words as *gem*, *jewel*, *diamond*, applied to valued human friends. In like manner, Christ is

* Rom. xii. 1. † Phil. ii. 17. ‡ Phil. iv. 18.
§ Heb. xiii. 15, 16. || 1 Peter ii. 5.

called in the Scriptures the *morning star*, the *temple*, and the *light* of heaven, and the like. Now a devout Jew would have been more likely to have borrowed such titles for the Saviour from the revered ritual, under which he had been born and educated, than from any other source. But the multitude and diversity of such titles, borrowed from the Jewish ritual, preclude any doctrinal inference, which might be drawn from the use of any one of them. He is called not only a *sacrifice*, in the sense of a slain victim; but also, '*a sacrifice, for a sweet-smelling savour*,' * that is, an incense-offering, — then again, the *mercy-seat*,† (for this, *all* sound commentators and critics admit, is the meaning of the word rendered *propitiation* in the *third* chapter of the Epistle to the Romans,) — then, the *high priest*, (frequently in the Epistle to the Hebrews,) — then also the *veil* between the holy place and the holy of holies.‡ Now all these analogies are true, beautiful, instructive, and edifying. They all open rich veins of devotional thought and feeling, and reflect back upon the Old Testament rays of gospel light, which cover it with the glory of the New, and shed around it the celestial halo, that encircled our Saviour's own brows. But you will see at once, that, if these analogies had been designed to represent doc-

* Eph. v. 2. † Rom. iii. 25. ‡ Heb. x. 20.

trinal facts, they could not all have been used. If, in a dogmatic point of view, Christ was a slain victim, he could not have been also an incense-offering, — if an offering, he could not have been also the mercy-seat, on which no offering was laid, — if a sacrifice, he could not have been also the high priest, who offered sacrifice. These comparisons, which, if anything more than figures, clash so harshly with each other, must then be regarded as mere images, designed to shadow forth, under various aspects, the power, the love, and the sufferings of Christ.

These figures occur chiefly in the Epistle to the Hebrews, which was written mainly to impress upon Jewish minds the spiritual majesty and beauty of Christianity. The Jewish converts missed, in Christianity, the outward beauty of holiness, to which they had been accustomed, the solemn tread of the priestly train, the pompous ceremonial of the great day of expiation, the smoke of the daily sacrifice. The writer of this epistle aimed to reconcile those, to whom he wrote, to the simplicity of the Christian system and ritual, by showing them, that, for everything beautiful and glorious in Judaism, Christianity offered something greater and more perfect of the same kind. The burden of the epistle is: ' God spake to the fathers *by the prophets ;* to us *by his Son.* Judaism has its *succession* of *dying* high priests, who must perform the same service over again *every year*; we have an *unchangeable* high priest, who remains *forever*, and whose *one* service and oblation is forever sufficient. Under the old dispensation, there was a tabernacle, glorious and beautiful, *made with hands*; ours is a greater and more perfect tabernacle, *not made with* hands.' Thus also, with numerous other particulars. If you will take this idea with you in reading the Epistle to the Hebrews, it will give that epistle a harmony and consistency, which you may not now, perhaps, be able to trace in it; and you will regard it as the very best form, in which Jewish prejudices could have been overcome, and the Christian faith of one born a Jew could have been conciliated or confirmed. This view of the epistle will account for much of the phraseology commonly quoted in the discussion of the atonement, and may prepare us for the consideration of particular texts upon this subject, to which I shall invite you in the next lecture.

My hour is fully spent; and I have spent it in negations, which I dislike to do, when it can be avoided. But on account of the tenacity with which many cling to the view, against which I have been contending, I have deemed it necessary to give it as thorough a discussion as possible, before presenting that view of the atonement, which seems to me both rational, Scriptural, and full of instruction and edification.

None can attach a higher efficacy than I would, to the cross and death of Christ; but I believe, (as I shall attempt to show you in the next lecture,) that it is, in the language of our text, 'God in Christ reconciling the world unto himself,' and not Christ reconciling God to man. As a sacrifice of love, in which God and Christ consent, may the Saviour's atoning blood be applied to our hearts and consciences, so that 'we, having received the atonement, may joy in God, through our Lord Jesus Christ.'

LECTURE VIII.

THE ATONEMENT.

1 PETER III. 18.

CHRIST ALSO HATH ONCE SUFFERED FOR SINS, THE JUST FOR THE UNJUST, THAT HE MIGHT BRING US TO GOD.

In my former lecture on THE ATONEMENT, I confined myself chiefly to the obvious considerations opposed to the doctrine of our Saviour's vicarious or substituted suffering. I showed you that this doctrine has no place in the recorded teachings of our Saviour, of his apostles, or of the early Christian fathers; that the forgiveness of the penitent was always a part of God's law; that the forgiveness of the penitent is not only consistent with perfect justice, but an essential part of justice; that Christ's vicarious sufferings destroy the doctrine of pardon, inasmuch as there can be no pardon, where the full penalty is paid; and that, so far from being an encouragement to sin, the free forgiveness of the penitent, and of those only, is the surest inducement to goodness. I then spoke of the absurdity of maintaining, as our Trinitarian brethren do, that God can punish God, or can be punished by God. I then showed you, that there are no traces, in the gospel history, of the infinite weight of agony said to have been laid upon our Saviour. I next exhibited the inconsistency of the vicarious atonement with some of our Saviour's principal statements of religious doctrine, — then too, with the immutability of the divine attributes. I then took up the frequent comparison of our Saviour to the Jewish sacrifices, on which rests perhaps the most frequently urged argument in favor of the vicariousness of his death. I showed you that the Jewish sacrifices were not vicarious; that Christ is more frequently compared to the paschal lamb, which was not even a sin-offering, than to any other part of the Jewish ritual; that comparisons with reference to his death are drawn indifferently from every portion of the Jewish ritual, which comparisons, if they designate doctrinal truths, are inconsistent with each other, and can be harmonized only by supposing them mere figures; and that the word *sacrifice*, with its corresponding phraseology, is employed with reference to a large variety of subjects and persons, other than Christ and his death. I now resume the subject; and may tax your patience for an unusual length of time, as I am solicitous to complete my discussion of the atonement this evening.

The advocates of the doctrine of vicarious suffering allege in its favor certain proof-texts, the principal of which we will now pass in cursory review. Many of these texts are, to my mind, entirely opposed to the doctrine, in behalf of which they are quoted; for they refer to Christ and his death, not as removing the punishment of sin, but as taking away sin itself, — an efficacy, which no Christian denies. Such are these texts: 'Behold the Lamb of God, which *taketh away the sin* of the world.'* 'The blood of Jesus Christ his Son *cleanseth us from all sin*.'† 'How much more shall the blood of Christ, who through the eternal spirit offered himself without spot to God, *purge your conscience* from dead works to serve the living God?'‡ These passages cannot imply vicarious punishment; for that does not take away sin, or have any effect upon the sinner, — it simply takes away the wrath of God and the penalty of his law. The taking away of sin is a work, which can be wrought only upon the individual's own soul and character, and with which a vicarious atonement has no possible connection. In point of fact, there is not a single text in the Bible, in which Christ is said to have taken away the punishment of men's sins, or to have appeased God's wrath, or to have made him propitious.

* John i. 29. † 1 John i. 7. ‡ Hebrews ix. 14.

I omit now the consideration of those texts, where Christ is merely spoken of as a *sacrifice;* for they were sufficiently discussed in the last lecture. I pass to the class of texts, in which Christ is said to *bear men's sins.* 'Who his own self *bear our sins* in his own body on the tree.' * In like manner, Isaiah says, 'Surely he hath *borne our griefs*, and *carried our sorrows;*' and, 'The Lord *hath laid on him*, (to be thus borne,) *the iniquity of us all.*' † We fortunately have in St. Matthew's gospel an authoritative interpretation of this phraseology. It is in the following passage: 'He cast out the spirits with his word, and healed all that were sick; that it might be fulfilled which was spoken by Esaias the prophet, saying, *Himself took our infirmities, and bare our sicknesses.*' ‡ He bore them by *bearing them off*, by *taking them away;* for no one of course supposes that he assumed the sicknesses, which he cured. In fact, in each of the original languages of the Scriptures, the word, which means to *lift* or *bear*, means also, and perhaps full as frequently, to *take off*, or to *carry away.*

Another class of texts is of those, in which the word *ransom* is employed. Our Saviour, as reported by Matthew and Mark, says: 'Whosoever will be chief among you, let him be your minister: even as the Son of man came, not to

* 1 Peter ii. 24. † Isaiah liii. 4, 6. ‡ Matt. viii. 16, 17.

be ministered unto, but to minister, and to give his life a *ransom* for many.'* St. Paul also says of Christ, that he 'gave himself a *ransom* for all.'† These are the only instances, in which the word occurs with reference to Christ. Now the word rendered *ransom* undoubtedly means, in its literal sense, *money paid to the captor for the redemption of a captive.* Is it contended that the word is used literally in the passage just quoted? Let those, who think so, tell us then, who was the captor of men's souls, and when and how any sum of money was paid to that captor. Do they say that there was no captor, and that no money was paid? Then they must acknowledge, that the word is figuratively employed with reference to our Saviour. But, if it be figuratively employed, we must look for its interpretation to its figurative use in the Bible on other subjects. Now the corresponding word, (both the noun and the verb,) is often used in the Old Testament with reference to the Israelites, in such a way that it can only denote the means or the act of *deliverance.* Thus, in Isaiah, God says to his covenant people, 'I gave Egypt for thy *ransom*,'‡ by which we cannot understand the price paid to those, who held the Israelites in captivity; for Egypt was the very power that kept Israel captive, and Egypt could not have

* Matthew xx. 27, 28; Mark x. 44, 45.
† 1 Timothy ii. 6. ‡ Isaiah xliii. 3.

been given to Egypt, but, on the other hand, was utterly subdued and spoiled. The sense obviously is: 'I gave up Egypt to defeat and humiliation for thy *deliverance.*' In like manner says Jeremiah: 'The Lord hath redeemed Jacob, and *ransomed* him from the hand of him that was stronger than he,' * that is, not *paid a price* for him, but manifestly *delivered* him. With reference to the Babylonish captivity, the Israelites are called the *ransomed*, and the *ransomed of the Lord*, by which is evidently meant, not *redeemed by the payment of a price*, but simply *delivered*. *Deliverance*, then, is the idea attached to the word *ransom*, when figuratively employed in the Bible; and, as it cannot be literally used with regard to our Saviour, I have not the slightest doubt, that the word means, as used with reference to his mediation, *deliverance from darkness, error, and sin.*

I would next refer to the texts, in which Christians are said to be *bought with a price.* There are two of these texts. The death of Christ is not spoken of in connection with either of them; and they both stand in such a connection, as to show that it is not the impunity, but the allegiance, the service of Christians, that is purchased. In one of them, the language is: 'He that is called, being free, is Christ's servant. Ye

* remiah xxxi. 11.

are *bought with a price;* be not ye the servants of men,'* that is, by what Christ has done and suffered in your behalf, he has purchased your service, — has laid upon you an imperative obligation to be the servants of no other master. The other text, in which this phrase occurs, relates to the duty of self-consecration to God's service. Know ye not that your body is the temple of the Holy Spirit which is in you, which ye have of God, and ye are not your own? For ye are *bought with a price;* therefore glorify God in your body, and in your spirit, which are God's.'† The obvious sense of this passage is, 'God, by the spiritual aid and grace, which he has bestowed upon you, has bought your allegiance, — has established an indefeasible claim to your service, — has made it your obvious and imperative duty to live, not as your own, but as his, as his in body, soul, and conduct.'

I next ask your attention to the texts, in which Christ is spoken of as a *propitiation.* They are three. One is in the Epistle to the Romans. 'Whom God hath set forth to be a *propitiation,* through faith in his blood, to declare his righteousness for the remission of sins that are past, through the forbearance of God: to declare, I say, at this time his righteousness, that he might be just, and the justifier of him which believeth

* 1 Corinthians vii. 22, 23. † 1 Corinthians vi. 19, 20.

in Jesus.'* This text, as a whole, is certainly opposed to the idea of vicarious suffering as the ground of pardon; for 'the remission of sins that are past' is expressly said to be, not through the sufferings of Christ, but 'through the forbearance of God,' and Jesus is said to be 'set forth' or manifested, not to make God merciful, but 'to declare' or exhibit 'his righteousness.' The word rendered *propitiation*, means *mercy-seat.* So say nearly all critics and commentators of any authority or value. This is one of the instances, in which our Saviour, by one who was born and educated a Hebrew of the Hebrews, is compared to a prominent portion of the religious apparatus of the Jews. The mercy-seat was the lid of the ark of the covenant. It was within the holy of holies. Above it were the cherubim. Upon it, and between their wings, rested, in the day of miracles, the luminous cloud, betokening the divine presence. On it was laid neither sacrifice nor offering. But, once a year, the high priest alone entered the holy of holies, sprinkled the blood of victims upon the mercy-seat, offered supplication for the divine forgiveness of the sins of the whole people, and came forth to declare to the assembled nation God's pardon to the penitent. How appropriately then is Jesus termed the mercy-seat, both as the fullest possible mani-

* Romans iii. 25, 26.

festation of the divine attributes, and as the messenger and pledge of the divine forgiveness! But the appropriateness of the comparison ceases, if you connect with it the idea of vicarious punishment. The true meaning of the rich and beautiful passage now under consideration may, perhaps, be discerned from the following paraphrase. 'Whom God has set forth as a mercy-seat through faith, [that is, a spiritual mercy-seat,] sprinkled, not with the blood of victims, but with his own blood, to exhibit or manifest in his own example the righteousness which he [God] requires, (for such was the forbearance of God, that, instead of visiting men's sins with desolating judgments, he sent his Son to take away sin,) to manifest in our own times the righteousness that God requires, that God might be just, might still adhere to that law, by which only the penitent are pardoned, and yet, that, through the beauty of Christ's example and the reconciling power of his cross, many might be led to repentance and a holy life, and might thus be accounted as righteous in his sight.'

The other two passages, in which the word *propitiation* is used, are these: 'If any man sin, we have an advocate with the Father, Jesus Christ the righteous, and he is the *propitiation* for our sins; and not for ours only, but for the sins of the whole world.'* 'Herein is love, not

* 1 John ii. 1, 2.

that we loved God, but that he loved us, and sent his Son to be the *propitiation* for our sins.'* In these texts the Greek word is not the same as that used in the text last under discussion; but it is a very similar word, derived from the same verb. It is the word employed in the Septuagint to designate the *sin-offerings* under the Jewish ritual; and this I suppose to be its meaning as used by St. John. These texts then are instances of yet another of the comparisons, so numerous in the New Testament, of Jesus and his death to features and portions of the religious ceremonial of the Jews. In my last lecture, I showed you that the Jewish sacrifices were not vicarious; and this being the case, the comparison of our Saviour to one of those sacrifices can be of no weight as an argument for the vicariousness of his atonement.

There are two or three single texts, which now demand our notice. One, which claims a passing comment on account of the frequency with which it is quoted, though it has no connection with the subject, is this: 'Without shedding of blood is no remission,'†—not, *of sins*, as it is usually quoted; for the sentence relates to the furniture of the tabernacle, which was of course incapable of sin. The word rendered *remission*, means *letting go*. The whole passage is: He,

* 1 John iv. 10. † Hebrews ix. 22.

[Moses,] sprinkled likewise with blood both the tabernacle, and all the vessels of the ministry. And almost all things are by the law purged with blood; and without shedding of blood is no *remission*,' that is, nothing is *let go*, is left, without being sprinkled with blood, — the simple statement of a well known fact in the Jewish economy, which an ignorant or careless person may indeed cite as referring to the death of Christ, but which I see not how a biblical scholar or a theologian could honestly quote as teaching one thing or another with regard to it.

Another passage is: 'He hath made him to be sin for us, who knew no sin, that we might be made the righteousness of God in him.' * I know of no commentator, who does not make *sin* here to denote a *sin-offering*. Among those, who give this exposition, I would mention Doddridge, McKnight, and Scott, all names of approved orthodoxy. Says McKnight on this verse, and with perfect truth, 'There are many passages in the Old Testament where *sin* signifies a sin-offering. Thus, Hosea iv. 8. *They* (the priests) *eat up the sin* (that is, the sin-offerings) *of my people*. In the New Testament, likewise, the word *sin* hath the same signification, Hebrews ix. 26, 28; xiii. 11.' The apostle's assertion then is, 'God has made him, who was

* 2 Corinthians v. 27.

sinless, to be a sin-offering for us, that we through him might be made righteous or holy.' Now, unless it can be proved that the sin-offerings under the Jewish dispensation were vicarious, the comparison of Christ to these sacrifices cannot indicate the vicariousness of his sufferings.

Another text, on which some reliance is placed, is this: 'Christ hath redeemed us from the curse of the law, being made a curse for us; for it is written, Cursed is every one that hangeth on a tree.'* The phrase, *being made a curse for us*, many regard as denoting, *becoming accursed of God for our sakes*, that is, bearing his wrath and indignation due to the guilt of man. But, on this point, I will quote a part of McKnight's note on the passage, simply saying, that I accord entirely with his view. 'Christ's dying on the cross is called *his becoming a curse*, that is, an accursed person, a person ignominiously punished as a malefactor; not because he was really a malefactor, and the object of God's displeasure, but because he was punished in the manner in which accursed persons, or malefactors, are punished. He was not a transgressor, but *he was numbered with the transgressors*. . . . . .
That this is the true import of the phrase *having become a curse*, is evident from the passage in the law, by which the apostle proves his asser-

* Galatians iii. 13.

tion: *It is written, accursed is every one who is hanged on a tree.'*

In addition to these passages, there are several in the New Testament, in which Christ is said to have *suffered or died for us*, or *for our sins*,—reiterations in fact of the prophet's words: 'He was wounded for our transgressions, he was bruised for our iniquities; the chastisement of our peace, (that is, the chastisement, through which our peace came,) was upon him; and with his stripes we are healed.'* These texts express, without ambiguity to my own mind, the great fundamental truth with regard to Christ's death, in which all Christians are agreed, namely, that he died for us, died in our behalf, and that his death is the means of our peace and happiness, both here and hereafter. They present no difficulty, they demand no forced interpretation, to make them consistent with the simplicity of our faith. Nay, it is only by a forced interpretation, that they are made to denote Christ's vicarious punishment. When you say that a patriot died for his country, that a self-devoted citizen suffered for the liberty or peace of his fellow-citizens, or that a missionary offered himself to privation, suffering, or death, for the ignorance or guilt of benighted pagans, you do not mean that one individual suffered or died in the

* Isaiah liii. 5.

stead of others; but simply, that he suffered in their behalf, and incurred death in his disinterested exertions for their good. Now why should we interpret the language of the Bible on different principles from those, on which we interpret other language? But all these complicated doctrines are founded on a broad departure from the common laws of interpretation, and on a stubborn determination to make words and phrases between the covers of the Bible mean something widely different from what they would mean in any other book. The phrases, which denote one's dying for another, when they occur elsewhere and on other subjects, are never deemed mystical. Why should any mystery hang over them, as we read them in the Bible?

I believe that I have now referred to the principal texts, or classes of texts, usually quoted by those, who believe that Christ was punished in our stead. I have not knowingly omitted any, which seemed to demand notice. In closing my remarks upon the doctrine of vicarious atonement, I would observe that the doctrine, if true, is not one, which there is any need of our knowing, or which can exert any practical influence upon our hearts or lives. If it be true, it is impossible, (as I showed you in the last lecture,) for us, in the present state of our faculties, to reconcile it with the justice of God; and the belief of it would therefore stand in the way of right feelings with reference to his character. And, if it be true, it simply indicates an effect, that was produced, two thousand years ago, on the divine mind,—a change, that was then wrought in the divine character. It teaches nothing with regard to our hearts or characters. It indicates no change to be wrought in us. A blood, shed to make God propitious, cannot be sprinked upon our hearts and consciences. We cannot be conscious of a penalty paid, or a punishment inflicted, in our behalf, ages before we were born. It can then make no essential difference, whether we believe this doctrine or not. The work, if wrought, may have been wrought for the benefit of us, who can trace no authentic records of it, no less than for that of the patriarchs and prophets of the infant world, who died before it was wrought. We may safely remain ignorant of what cannot possibly affect our hearts or lives. It can be of no vital consequence for us to know those things only, by knowing which we may be led to do what we should otherwise leave undone, or to omit what we should otherwise do. Tried by this test, Christ's punishment in our stead, whether true or false, cannot claim the place usually assigned to it, among essential, fundamental doctrines. The denial of it, if it do not, (as I believe that it does,) enhance the obligation to gratitude, penitence, and holiness, at least leaves the obligation to those duties unimpaired.

I now proceed to give a brief exposition of my own views of the atonement. The three great points, which seem to me to characterize the Scriptural doctrine of the atonement, are, *first*, that *God is the author; secondly*, that *man is the object;* and, *thirdly*, that *holiness is the end of the atonement.* These three ideas are found combined in very many of the instances, in which the mission, mediation, and death of Christ are spoken of in the New Testament. I will read two or three passages of this nature, as specimens of scores that I might quote.

'*God* was in Christ, *reconciling the world unto himself.*' * *God*, the author; *the world*, the object; *reconciliation to himself*, that is, holiness, the end.

'*God* hath made him to be sin *for us*, who knew no sin, *that we might be made the righteousness of God* in him.' † *God*, the author; *for us*, the object; *that we might be made the righteousness of God*, the end.

Where God is not mentioned in the very sentence, in which our Saviour's mission, mediation, or death, is spoken of, still the end, the production of holiness in man, is in hardly a single instance omitted. How clearly is this end, in contradistinction to any purpose with reference to the disposition or character of God, expressed in the following passages: 'Christ hath also

* 2 Corinthians v. 19. † 2 Corinthians v. 21.

once suffered for sin, the just for the unjust, *that he might bring us to God.*' * 'Our Saviour Jesus Christ, who gave himself for us, *that he might redeem us from all iniquity, and purify unto himself a peculiar people, zealous of good works.*' † 'Christ Jesus came into the world *to save sinners.*' ‡ 'Who his own self bare our sins in his own body on the tree, *that we, being dead to sin, should live unto righteousness.*' §

The leading idea of the Scriptural doctrine of the atonement then is, that Christ died to make men holy, to reconcile them to God, to lead them to his love and service, to make them 'followers of God as dear children;' in fine, that Christ died, to work, not upon God, but upon man, and for him to perform, not an outward, but an inward service, — a service, the efficacy of which is upon the human heart and character.

I am well aware that many represent this as an inferior work, — as a work, which needed not for its discharge a personage so eminent and heavenly, and which can hardly have authorized the strong language used in the Bible in regard to Christ's death, or the exalted titles and homage ascribed to Jesus on earth and in heaven. Had I not often heard this objection, I should think it no compliment to your spiritual discern-

* 1 Peter iii. 18. † Titus ii. 10, 11.
‡ 1 Timothy i. 15. § 1 Peter ii. 24.

ment to take notice of it; for I feel sure that I have your entire sympathy, when I say that the greatest service, which God himself can render to man, is to make him holy, perfect, godlike, to redeem him from the power of sin, and to shed the consecration of a devout and dutiful spirit over his whole soul and his whole life. And if Christ has performed this service for man, then has he performed for him the most momentous and godlike service possible, — a service, for which he cannot but have a name above every other name, and for which the eternal ascription of gratitude and praise must echo through the ranks of the redeemed. Leave this service unperformed, leave me in unrepented sin, with my grovelling aims and unconsecrated life, and it is a small service, that a price is paid, or a penalty borne in my stead, — I carry my hell about with me, a hell, which would shed its blackness over my spirit, were I in paradise. But save me from my sins, purge my conscience, sanctify my soul, reform and consecrate my life, in hell itself I should be proof against its torments, — I cannot but be happy, — my heaven is within, and cannot be taken from me. The idea, that to elevate and sanctify the inner man is a subordinate work, proceeds from the unspiritual, grovelling ways of thinking, that have been but too characteristic of our race taken collectively. Men most admire what comes with observation, —

what is external and formal. They appreciate not what is wrought in the hidden man of the heart, and ripens for eternity. On this ground, the conqueror has always seemed a greater man than the philanthropist, and the founder of a hospital, than he, who heals the diseases of the soul. On precisely the same principle is it, that men have assigned a higher dignity and worth to an atonement, which should wipe away all punishment at a single stroke, than to an atonement, which must be wrought over afresh in each individual heart, creating it anew in the beauty of holiness and in the fulness of the divine image. To my own mind, the latter office with regard to the individual soul is the highest office, which I can imagine as belonging to the Saviour; and to say that the blood of Christ has cleansed a single soul from sin, and has wholly sanctified that soul, is to ascribe more to it, than were we to say that it has removed the mere penalty of violated law from a whole universe of sinners.

But some one may say: 'If Christ does no more than to cleanse the soul from sin, and to renew it in the divine image, my hope of pardon for my past sins is gone.' It is gone, I reply, if you will persist in looking upon God as essentially vindictive and unforgiving; but not, if you will only take God's testimony concerning his own character, uttered many ages before Christ died, when he revealed himself to Moses, 'The

Lord, the Lord God, merciful and gracious, long-suffering, and abundant in goodness and truth, keeping mercy for thousands, forgiving iniquity, and transgression, and sin.' I believe that God was never otherwise than he then declared himself. I build no more than those, who hold an opposite doctrine, on my own merits. I depend for forgiveness on the eternal mercy of God, made known to the fathers, made manifest and incarnate in Christ. Let none call this a sandy foundation. If God's mercy be not a sufficient basis for our trust, I know not what can suffice. It is a foundation broader than the universe, — immovable, though heaven and earth pass away. It belts creation with a zone of love. It upholds all worlds and beings. It is boundless and infinite. The need, so often expressed of Christ's vicarious punishment, is a need, which the doctrine itself creates. I should feel it, if I believed that God was ever unwilling or unable to forgive. I should feel it, if I believed, in Doctor Watts's language, that God's throne 'once was a seat of dreadful wrath,' and that '*Vengeance* was his name.'

But let it not be supposed that I do not connect Christ, his sufferings, and his death, most intimately with the forgiveness of sins. My hope of pardon is in God through Christ. The doctrine of pardon, even if revealed before Christ, was not so brought to light and made manifest, that it could be the object of a sustaining and satisfying faith. On the question, whether God will forgive sin, the analogies of nature shed no light; for her subtle powers and majestic agencies have never sinned, but are all obedient. Those, therefore, who have been left to the light of nature, have never found peace under the burden of transgression; but have gone the whole round of fasts, penances, pilgrimages, and self-tortures, without obtaining through any or all of these means the assurance of forgiveness. Nor did the fainter and often mysterious light of God's earlier revelations communicate this assurance in its fulness. To the heart that knows itself, and feels its unworthiness and sinfulness, the most vital of all questions is, Can I be forgiven? And to this question, no sufficient and satisfying answer has been afforded, except in the loving and paternal attributes of the Almighty, as made manifest in the person, the ministry, the cross of Christ. But, when we look to Jesus as the image of God, we behold in him a love full and free, ready to forgive, waiting to be gracious. We feel that there is no limit to the mercy, which, amidst the agonies of death, could make intercession for the transgressors; and we can thus look for pardon with implicit confidence to that mercy on the throne of the universe, which he, who on the cross prayed for his murderers, came to declare and manifest. It is then to God, as revealed and beheld in Christ, that we look for pardon. But we regard the promise and pledge of pardon, as but the means and motive to personal holiness. Jesus says to us, 'Your sins be forgiven,' only that he may add, with an emphasis, which pardoning mercy alone could send home to the soul of the penitent, 'Go, and sin no more.' God permits us to behold his forgiving love in Christ, that, through the energy of this love, our souls may be transformed, renewed, and sanctified.

But in behalf of a vicarious atonement, I have sometimes heard an appeal made to personal experience. Let us then analyze experience, and see how far it can go. There are many here, I trust, who have personally 'received the atonement,' who cherish the faith and hope, and lead the life of the Christian, who feel the peace of God in their hearts, and breathe his spirit in their daily conversation. Were I addressing myself to an individual of this class, I should appeal to his own consciousness, and say, What, my friend, are you conscious that Christ has done for you? That he has paid any price for you? That he has incurred any penalty due to you? No. Of this, even if it be the case, you cannot be conscious. Of what, then, are you conscious? That Christ has made the name of God a dear and cherished name to your heart;

that he has brought you near to him, as a child to a Father; that he has taught you to pray; that he has made you love virtue; that he has led you, drawn you on, in the path of duty; that his cross and death have appealed to your best affections, have rebuked your selfishness and worldliness, have made you feel the beauty of holiness, have been to your soul a touching manifestation of divine love, have laid you under a pleasing constraint to live, not for yourself, but for him that died for you. You have looked upon the cross, and said, 'Herein is love;' and that love has made the yoke of obedience easy, and the burden of duty light, has called out your own love, has made you heartily penitent for sin, and earnestly desirous to live as the cross bids you live, and to be a follower of the Lamb whithersoever he goeth. This is the sum of the Christian's religious experience,—this, the atonement wrought in the true disciple's heart, — this, the work which takes precedence of all others, in its dignity, its worth, and its fruits.

Let us now pause for a moment, and consider how much is implied in that one word, *atonement,—reconciliation.* Here is a human being, either sunk in gross depravity, or immersed in the heartless pursuit of gain or pleasure. He is alienated from God, renders him no thanks, offers him no prayers, and lives as he might live, were he self-created and in a world of his own. His sympathies are either shut up within his own bosom, or flow within the narrow channel of home and kindred; and, even for those whom he loves, he seeks not the best gifts, loves not their souls, — his love may be false, fatal to their highest interests, — he may wreathe around them his own chains of worldliness or guilt, — his example and influence may be pestilential to all within his reach. For that man atonement is to be made. He is to be brought to God. Those stains upon his spirit and his life are to fade away before the light of God's countenance. That soul must look on Jesus, till his divine features stamp themselves upon it. That heart, so cold, or so filled with lower loves, must be wholly filled with the love of God. That life, so selfish, must breathe a diffusive, all-embracing charity. That example, that influence, now neutral, if not baneful, must bless all on whom it shines, and lead neighbors, friends, strangers, to give glory to God for its beautiful light. The whole character must reflect the divine image. There must be a reconciliation of will and purpose, a blending of the man's will with his God's, a oneness of aim and effort, a frame of soul and of life, of which the man may say with truth, 'God dwells in me, and I in him.' Not until all this is the case, not until the Father's love throbs in every pulsation of the child's heart, and the Father's will rules in every action of the child's life, is the atonement, the *at-one-ment*, fully made.

It is this high and glorious work, which Jesus performs, when he brings us to the Father, when he reconciles us unto God. This is the atonement, of which God is the author, Christ the agent, man the object. To effect this was the whole work of Christ's ministry, miracles, teachings, life, death, resurrection, and intercession. But, in this work, the New Testament assigns the most prominent place to the death of Christ; and every Christian heart assigns to it the same place. He is no Christian, to whom the cross is not dear, and who has not felt the need and worth of a suffering Redeemer. The blood of Calvary has been the life-blood of the Church.

For, in the first place, it is by love, that man, when alienated from God, is softened, humbled, and made penitent. He could resist threats. He could steel his heart against the denunciations of vengeance. In the fearful might of a rebellious spirit, he could dare a frowning heaven and a vindictive Deity. But love has a voice, to which none can listen unmoved, especially when it makes itself heard from amidst torture and mortal agony, incurred in behalf of those with whom it pleads. How does the thought of one, who suffered and died for every man, rouse the last faint spark of virtuous feeling and of moral strength, and fan it into a generous flame! How does it bring near, those who were afar off, make them ashamed of their wanderings, and excite the earnest longing, that for themselves such love may not have been in vain! 'Greater love hath no man than this, that a man lay down his life for his friends.' Jesus might have dwelt on earth in glorious majesty, and passed to heaven from an unsuffering ministry, and yet have loved man no less; but man would not have discerned the depth, or felt the power of his love, had he not gone as a lamb to the slaughter, and freely given himself up for us all.

But was it his own love only, that Jesus manifested on the cross? No; but also the love of One greater than he. For he came from the bosom of the Father; and he represented his own mission and death as the fruit, the expression, the pledge of the Father's love. 'God so loved the world, that he gave his only begotten Son.' In him was manifested the fulness of the Godhead bodily: and, in the depth of his compassion and the perfectness of his love, he was exhibiting the intensity of God's pity, and the fervor of his affection for his human family. By carrying his love to the last point of endurance and of sacrifice, he exhibited the boundlessness of that mercy, which is the sinner's hope, — he made the promise of pardon full, free, all-embracing, — he bore the image of a Father always ready to forgive, always waiting to be gracious. 'Scarcely for a righteous man will one die; yet peradventure for a good man some would even dare to die. But God commendeth his love towards us, in that while we were yet sinners, Christ died for us.' When we look at the cross, we are constrained to ask, with St. Paul: 'He that spared not his own Son, but delivered him up for us all, how shall he not with him also freely give us all things?' When we view God in Christ, as Christ seals his mission with his blood, we can exclaim, with the same apostle: 'I am persuaded that neither death, nor life, nor angels, nor principalities, nor powers, nor things present, nor things to come, nor height, nor depth, nor any other creature, shall be able to separate us from the love of God, which is in Christ Jesus our Lord.' It is in the love and the cross of Christ, that the Father goes forth to meet the wandering child. It is in Christ crucified, that he reveals the fulness of paternal love; and thus, from the first moment, gives the penitent broad, firm ground for encouragement and hope, without which he would have neither confidence nor strength to retrace his evil ways, and to return to the path of God's commandments.

Then, too, it behoved Christ, as our guide and example in duty, as the *way* and the *life*, to be *made perfect through suffering*. His godlike purity and virtue might have been no less perfect and entire in a manifestation, without suffering, and full of outward glory. But the beauty of the picture would have been marred by the gold and tinsel of its setting. It shows itself most perfect and divine, when encompassed by no outward form or comeliness, wrapped in the weeds of sorrow, and shining forth from the shadow of death. His submission, his tenderness, his forgiveness, his philanthropy, his piety, could have had, in no other form, their full manifestation. His example could have been, under no other circumstances, so radiant with spiritual beauty, so attractive, so inviting. It is at the cross, that we learn the full preciousness and loveliness of Christ's character, and feel ourselves the most loudly called, the most tenderly entreated, to become his followers.

Then also Christ's sufferings and death bring his example home to those scenes of trial, conflict, sorrow, and agony, in which we are the most strongly tempted to forsake the service of God, and in which, therefore, we stand in the most urgent need of divine help and strength. We behold in him a full and perfect victory over every enemy to our peace and progress. We see the sting of sorrow destroyed, the power of death subdued. We behold him triumphant over grief, and agony, and the bitterness of the grave; and trace, through the shadow of his tomb, a path of living light that leads to heaven.

We hear from his cross the voice, 'Be thou faithful unto death, and I will give thee a crown of life;'—'To him that overcometh will I grant to sit with me in my throne, even as I also overcame, and am set down with my Father in his throne.'

In all these points of view, was Christ's death an essential part of that plan of redemption, by which man is saved from sin, and made one with God. Without his death, his own love would not have been fully shown, and might have pleaded in vain. Without his death, God's love in him would not have had its utmost manifestation; God's promise of pardon through him would have lacked its seal; God's invitation, his offered mercy to the returning sinner, would not have had full emphasis of utterance. Without his death, his example would have wanted its most godlike aspects. Without his death, his example would not have applied itself to those scenes and seasons of life, in which we are the most liable to faint or to wander, and the most in need of divine light and guidance. His death, then, was essential to the full power of the gospel, and thus to the restoration and sanctification of the human soul.

Yet, because I deem Christ's death thus essential, I do not undervalue his life, his teachings, his resurrection, or his intercession. They all combine to constitute the vast and beautiful system of means, by which God reconciles man to himself, and through which man receives the atonement.

If these things be so, brethren, the atonement is a work wrought, not for us, but within us. It is Christ's work of grace in our souls. When we feel in our inmost hearts, and show forth in our daily walk and conversation, the power of his death, the power of his spirit; when the cross is reërected in our souls, and our sins are nailed to it; when his last prayer, 'Father, into thy hands I commend my spirit,' is the prayer of our whole lives; then, and not till then, have we received the atonement. Let our discussion awaken us all to self-examination as to our part in this work of grace, in this inward salvation. And let us account 'Christ formed within' as our only hope of glory; and deem ourselves his, only so far as we bear the image of his purity, submission, obedience, love, and piety.

I have now, my friends, in a series of *eight* lectures, reviewed with you some of the heads of Christian doctrine, on which I dissent from the established creeds of those portions of the church, with which, next to our own, we are the most conversant. In my *first* lecture, I labored to establish the *divine unity.* In my *second,* I discussed the question of *our Saviour's supreme divinity.* In my *third,* I endeavored to exhibit a comprehensive view of the teaching of Scripture with regard to *Christ's true rank and dignity.* My *fourth* was upon the *nature and agency of the Holy Spirit.* My *fifth* was on *human nature;* my *sixth*, on *regeneration;* my *seventh* and *eighth* have been on the *atonement.* There are other points of Christian doctrine, which I wish to present in similar systematic and argumentative discourses; and, particularly, I hope, at some future time, should my life be spared, to present to you, in a course of sermons, the *positive* side of our views of Christian truth, without reference to points in controversy. But other engagements dispose me now to close the present course, especially as I have embraced in it a group of subjects, which naturally belong together, and so connect themselves with each other, as to give to the course a certain unity and wholeness.

In conclusion, let me urge you, on all these subjects, to search the Scriptures for yourselves, diligently and prayerfully, and not to accept my results, without making them your own, by the careful use of the reason with which God has endowed you, and the light which he has given you. And may he, the spirit of truth, guide you into all truth, and make you faithful in the way of his commandments, even in that path, which grows brighter and brighter unto the perfect day.

www.ingramcontent.com/pod-product-compliance
Lightning Source LLC
LaVergne TN
LVHW010241110826
845151LV00004B/1362

* 9 7 8 1 4 2 5 5 2 4 2 8 9 *